A Mother's Heart

Angels, Awakening, Loss and Healing

Valerie Inanna

A Mother's Heart: Angel, Awakening and Healing Copyright 2020 by Valerie Inanna. All rights reserved. No part of this book may be used or reproduced in any manner whatsoever, including Internet usage, nor may it be stored in a retrieval system, transmitted, translated into another language without written permission from of Valerie Inanna, except in the case of brief quotations embodied in critical articles and reviews.

Cover design and illustrations by Valerie Inanna

Editing by Jo Eager

Interior photos by Valerie Inanna

Note: This book is not meant to substitute advice from of a licensed professional. This book is sold with the understanding that the author and publisher are not engaged in rendering medical or health services.

Library of Congress Cataloging-in-Publication Data

TXu 2-215-072

Inanna, Valerie, 1957-

A Mother's Heart: Angels, Awakening and Healing/ Valerie Inanna.

First Edition

First Printing, 2020

-

ISBN 978-1-7355857-0-3

1.   1. Mothers 2. Spiritual 3. Angels 4. Loss 5. Healing

Dedicated to my sons, Michael and Nathan.
Thank you for being the teachers of my heart.
I will love you for all time.

INTRODUCTION

If the concepts in this book are new to your way of thinking, thank you for taking the time to explore it. The idea of hearing Angels may seem beyond your imagination. Before it happened to me, I'd been talking to them all my life without hearing them. It had been more of a one-sided conversation to help get me through childhood events. The idea of being heard was comforting.

What if you were open to communicating with angels when you needed support? What would happen if you listened? Some people may sense them in ways beyond hearing; you may sense an angels' presence or just feel it in your heart. Trusting that they are there is a great gift to allow yourself.

I was blessed with two sons. They had distinct different personalities and how they looked at life. Like us, our children come here to have experiences. There are lessons. My boys were the heart lessons that I did not expect. Only when we love so deeply can another person change or affect your life and growth. Instead of me being their teacher, they were mine. I am forever changed because of them.

Loss and the process of grieving can be devastating to all systems of our Being: body, mind, Spirit and Soul. Pain may block or breakdown one of those systems. Moving beyond it may seem impossible in the moment. Trust that you will. Only in moving forward will you discover healing. This is the story of my growth in life and heart lessons.

We all hold onto moments from life, some joyful, some painful. You can find wisdom in both. How we choose to hold it is the difference.

This is my experience. Everyone will have their own viewpoint happening in a same moment. One does not outweigh another. Each person has a unique take on what happens and how it affects them. That's the beauty in life's experiences.

We can only tell our story, through our view. This is mine.

A Mother's Heart

Contents

Chapter 1   Awakening

Chapter 2   Halloween 15

Chapter 3   Beginning 19

Chapter 4   Angels 29

Chapter 5   Love 40

Chapter 6   Trauma 62

Chapter 8   Choosing to Heal 69

Chapter 9   A Mother's Heart 90

Chapter 10   Messages 107

Chapter 11   Eight Years Later 112

Chapter 12   Putting Pieces Together 121

Chapter 13   Heart Healing Further 130

Chapter 14   Transmission of Love 136

Chapter 15   Letter..................................... 148

Chapter 16   What's Next & Book Cover 154

Awakening

How can anyone receive a Divine Transmission and ever be the same again? It came unexpectedly and with no warning. Immersed in a Light I had only ever imagined might be possible. Simply put, I physically felt an all-encompassing Light, all that is GOD, holding me. Touching into the vastness of all that is Love, it felt profound and eternal.

The depth of this support was nothing I had ever experienced—a true peace that calmed me. Connecting into an inner knowing that I easily speak of today, then it was all new. This quiet and stillness allowed my ears and heart to listen and understand. Although it was years ago, it's still so clear, happening all again as I write.

It was a typical fall evening in 1985 in southern California. The kids were in bed together. Michael, the oldest, would read stories until his little brother, Nathan, who was four years younger, closed his eyes.

With a sense of accomplishment, he'd close his own eyes, feeling good about the day.

My husband and I were lying on our sides on the sofa watching TV. I was in front of him. Very tired, it felt good as he held me close. All was right in the world.

Something began to feel different in the room. Doubting what I was feeling, I figured it was fatigue. A soft ringing started; I was receiving it in my right ear. It was gently high-pitched, beginning in waves. It wasn't like a bell or anything I've heard on earth. The TV screen became what we called as kids, tunnel vision. Depth perception shifts between you and an object. That's what was happening. The screen and voices felt so far away, smaller. As I watched the reduced version the images of the actors faded, static replaced them. Their voices moved from clear to scratchy until they disappeared.

It was as if my personal tuner was being adjusted into something I was not conscious of before that moment. The images had faded into static, horizontal lines across the screen. Between the lines, a bright, constant Light was shining. I have no recollection of time. Without effort, the static cleared into pure light, drawing all focus from me.

A brilliant white light emitting from inside the screen filtered out, resembling a mist around the TV. I have no recollection of feeling my body or my husband's, with his arm wrapped around me. Instead, I felt the Light wrapped around me with a feeling of safety like I'd never felt before. It was all there was.

Waves of sound seemed to change, like tuning into a clear channel on the radio. As this happened, the center of the white light became golden. Not a metallic gold, it was purity. My heart felt it! The golden light surrounded by white no longer stayed within the TV.

The Light was being drawn to me or me to it. Parts of me that I did not understand at that time felt new expressions of awareness. Clarity and awakening happened swiftly. The waves tuned in and became a language that I deciphered as Waves of Love.

"Oh my God, this is of GOD," I thought! This outpouring of Love allowed me to completely relax, be held, and listen. Something was going to happen. This emission made me feel that I'd have all the support needed to get through something. This voice, coming as waves of love, directed me that this would be the deepest loss I could ever imagine. A new wave came and I accepted it, feeling complete trust. "All was going to be okay" no matter what was about to happen. Over and over, as if I needed to take it in on many more unconscious levels. There was support for me and I knew it with my whole heart and Being. Over and over, the love came, reassuring me. Other bits and pieces came to me, but nothing seemed more important than "ALL WOULD BE OKAY." Inside I knew this without a doubt. "All would be okay."

In this concrete knowing, the waves of Love that had traveled across the room to the sofa began to pull back into the TV. Efficiently, the voice frequency moved back into waves, quieting the new language. The static returned briefly as the light left the screen, my ears no longer hearing the ringing. Once again, the room was as it had been—back to what I knew as "normal." The actors were back in focus on the TV, theirs voices now clear. My husband was behind me, his arm still around me. I lay still trying to just breathe and figure out what just happened. How long had it been?

Turning on the sofa to face him, I asked him if he had witnessed anything. My voice sounded strange. He said no, the TV didn't change and he hadn't heard the ringing. He did feel a change in me during that time. I shared with him all that had just transpired in our family room. Emotional from the experience, I cried, relaying as much detail as I could.

"Do you think I'm losing my mind?" I asked.

"No," he replied, holding me close. He told me I looked different. He believed that it was guidance from the Angels, GOD.

The event was on my mind throughout the next

week. I tried to figure out the most devastating thing that could happen. I concluded that it was a Divine loving warning, preparing me for the death of one of my parents. The love feeling never left me from that day. Even a week later I felt held and was so grateful for this support. I could breathe knowing all would be okay.

Every day, I waited for that dreadful phone call I'd been prepared for. A call to inform me that a parent across the country was dead. It was sad to think about, a sense of heart mourning began. And each time I would remember a voice saying, "All Would Be Okay."

Halloween

It was the week of Halloween. The house was decorated with cutouts the kids made, along with store-bought pumpkins and bones. Trick-or-treat bags ready, costumes chosen, candy bought.

Fall in California is beautiful. So many colors of flowers and blooms in the air. Back east, we had fall colors and dried leaves. In California, we enjoy bright pink bougainvillea, green grass, and smells of something exotic and new opening.

Michael, my oldest, was loving kindergarten and all it brought. My husband was a runner and Michael wanted to be a part of that. Before breakfast they would run a half mile or so, return home to breakfast, then off to school.

One morning after the regular run, Michael sat at the table and complained of a headache. He didn't often complain so when he threw up it seemed reasonable to keep him home from school. He became upset and insisted he go to school. The headache passed and he was no longer sick to his stomach, so I let him go. The next morning, I asked that they not push so hard on the run. Again, upon returning, Michael complained of a headache and threw up. I asked my husband if there were some flowers or plants along the route that Michael could be allergic to. This was our first fall in this part of the country. Flowers, weeds, everything was different. If this allergy is affecting him so strongly, I felt a doctor's appointment was needed. The nurse got us in that afternoon. Still, I was waiting for the dreaded call about my parents.

After a brief exam by the doctor, the nurse returned with an address on a slip of paper for us to go for a CAT Scan, immediately.

Naive and without question, I followed the orders given. A young female technician led us into the room where the scan would be taken. Her voice was gentle as she helped Michael get comfortable on the table in such an unfamiliar atmosphere.

Curious, I asked the tech if I could look over her shoulder to watch the process. How fascinating to see the inside of Michael's brain. How could they tell allergies from that? I wondered. The images appeared on the screen. The tech explained which was the front of the head, the eye sockets, and other areas, so I could better understand what I was looking at. His brilliant brain exposed in black, white, and grays.

"What is that in the back of his brain," I asked.

Silence. I asked again, thinking she didn't hear me. Again, silence.

She went to get my son off the table without a word. She left us alone, returning a few minutes later. She told us to return to the doctor's office, so we headed back across town.

Back at the pediatrician's office, a nurse took Michael into a waiting area. The doctor took me into a small room and closed the door.

"Michael has a brain tumor." Boom, that was it!

No words to prepare, no kindness, no have a seat, let's talk. I was standing and she changed my family's life forever in one sentence. "Michael has a brain tumor." Still today, tears run down my face as they did that day. The doctor may have said she was sorry as she handed me a tissue and an address to an Oncology Children's Hospital about an hour drive away.

"The neurologist and oncologist will be seeing Michael today after you get registered." "Registered? I asked. "We are going to the hospital and stay overnight?"

The doctor looked at me and said, "You had to know it was a brain tumor." Yes, those were her words.

"How am I supposed to think that when my son has a headache, he has a brain tumor?" I asked quietly in a state of shock. It was all blurring together. The doctor's words felt so cold, uncaring, and unreal. Panic and the heat of it were welling inside.

Then I remembered, "All would be ok

Beginning

The transmission that came to prepare me before the life I knew ended--was it Angels? Was it GOD? Does it matter if we know? I believe it was. That's what my heart says. I trusted that day when the TV screen changed and a new world of understanding was opened to me. I am forever grateful for it. It did not end with the discovery of the brain tumor in my five-year-old son's brain stem.

The messages continued to come when things were about to get bad. Visions of these Angels became so clear. I learned what third eye vision meant. These Beings who spoke to me in the language of pure love were sending me a Divine Loving message to carry me through times I may not have been able to make it through on my own. They held me up and made me stronger than I could ever have imagined. People would comment that I was the strongest person they knew.

"It's not me, it's GOD and the Angels," I would reply. The Angels knew I was not awakened enough to handle what was ahead on my own. What a loving gift to have a team that was created for us to get through each day.

The following day, Michael was asleep in intensive care following his first surgery. It was for a shunt. He had developed hydrocephalus, fluids gathering on the brain, caused by a block created from the tumor. That is what was causing him to throw up after activity. A shunt was put in his brain to drain the fluid down into his stomach with a tube placed under the skin, the first step in many dealing with a benign pediatric cerebral astrocytoma.

My education was just beginning in many things besides Angels. It was an introduction to terms never used in my vocabulary before. Astrocytoma? It is a type of tumor that has feelers like arms coming from it that can grow and reach around and into places. My son's invader had formed an egg size mass in his cerebellum and reached out to wrap in and around his brain stem. After Michael's recovery from his shunt surgery, this issue would be addressed. For now, the focus was him, now in ICU.

The visiting pastor, the hospital's child psychologist, and I stood at the bottom of Michael's bed talking softly, waiting to see the doctor. It had been an exceptionally long day, night, and day again. I was tired. As we talked, I glanced over at Michael. What took me by surprise was what was over him and over the bed. At first my brain didn't want to register it. The Light was bright, yet gently soft. There was no heat from it, but it lit the space. Looking closer, it was an Angel! A huge, bright, white Angel formed directly over Michael's head and up to the ceiling.

My mind wondered if I was really seeing it. I turned to the two standing physically close to me, to see their reaction. They continued chatting. There was no sign that they saw anything. I must be seeing things. I looked back again. There it was holding steady above Michael. This time I noticed the glow surrounded Michael's head, too. Okay, I thought and turned back to the pastor and Hilda, the child psychologist. We had spoken throughout the day so there was enough comfort level for me to include them.

"I don't want you to think I am losing my mind," I said. "I know I'm tired. There is an Angel over Michael's bed."

They both looked and then turned back to me. " I believe you," they said in unison.

They didn't see the Angel that day, but they could see my face. I'm sure it's a common occurrence and this was just new for me. Right? Their answers were perfect. I was so grateful for them being there.

The Angel's presence settled my mind. It was a loving way to have my eyes opened to a world with them. Michael was being looked after. It was made perfectly clear that day.

It somehow made it easier as a mother. The message I received was backed up with a real Angel! I had no idea that day all that would be coming in the future. Was it the state of being I was in—vulnerable, exhausted, in such a state of prayer for Michael? Was it all of the people praying, who'd heard about the tumor within hours of the diagnosis? It was through word of mouth—we didn't have cell phones or text at the time.

Looking back, it seems orchestrated by GOD, with everything put in place for that day and the years to come. It wasn't easy. Yet, each time something new or different happened, it was as if an alert went off and the Angels appeared. In my heart, I know they were carrying us all, every day. I don't know how I would have made it without them. The Angels get the credit for handling this huge task of watching over Michael and me. Thank you so much for showing yourselves, for everything. I love you.

At such a young age, Michael endured so much: years of surgeries, tumor removal, shunt corrections over and over, more tumors, brain surgeries requiring therapy afterward to regain hand and arm control, for his legs to walk, and his speech, radiation, steroids time and time again, pain, having his spine completely fused, losing 90percent of his hearing, kidney stones, skin cancer, seizures, many decubitus skin ulcers, all the bladder infections, diabetes, MRSA. All of that, and I've probably missed a few.

Through it all, he remained Michael. When there's trauma at a young age, we get a bit stuck in that time. His innocence remained in his child like sense of humor and hope. He was very bright. The child psychologist at the hospital studied and tested him, concluding he had an IQ of 149. He could talk to any adult with ease at the age of five.

The psychologist became a friend over the years of hospital stays, visits and therapies. She suggested Michael and I write a book about our experiences, acknowledging the bond we had and that our story may help others. Michael and I talked about it as he grew older. He decided he never wanted to relive this experience in a shared book. It would have been an amazing story to read through his eyes. His take on all of it may have helped someone on their journey. As it stands, he taught and helped people grow every day of his life. I understand not wanting to put it all behind and move on. There was so much pain; not something you want to relieve. For many years, I didn't want to open up my heart and share everything, but now I am guided to write.

Along with these horrific things happening in Michael's body was the bright side—the connection that opened around him to Source/God/Creator and Angels. Through his worst hardships came my awakening into a world of new understanding. I struggled with this. I was becoming more aware and complete, as he went through so much suffering. It didn't seem fair and as his mom, I would have gladly taken on his pain. And yet, that wasn't how it was set up. Michael was the strong warrior, and I was learning through him. Thank you, Michael. I love you.

From day one, we were a team. We were strong together and did not doubt. He trusted me completely and I would give my life for him. Our Soul connection was beyond most parent-child expressions and we were both okay with that. It may have been put in place because of all that was going to be happening in his lifetime. Whatever the reason, I am grateful every day that we could be there for each other.

I feel there are two parts of me having this entire experience. The Spiritual side of me is learning and growing by leaps and bounds, feeling the Light and Love in all things. Then there is the earthly side that has been weighted down by my own life experiences and everything the world throws at you. My heart lives in both. It celebrates the joys in connection and feels the pain of it breaking at the same time.

When I heard that Michael had six months to live, all the joy inside of me ended, everything dulled. On the outside you need to perform so your children can have some sense of normal. Normal is an overrated word. What does that really mean? My new normal was to look in every morning to see if my sweet son was alive. Every morning I would stand at his door and watch to see if he was still breathing. I held my breath waiting to see his.

To start your day in unknowing wears on your heart. When he began snoring, it became a favorite sound. Walking down the hall in the morning hearing a snore come from his room made it a great day, no matter what else we had to deal with. It's funny how people complain of that sound. For me, it means life.

Over the years, before each medical occurrence, a warning message would come. Not like the first time with the TV. Now, I would sense a change and hear the sounds that translated somehow into words I could understand. It always felt there was an adjustment happening to accommodate my understanding.

Never did I doubt it. My faith in Creator/GOD/Source had never let me down or alone in any part of this. When the message came, I'd switch into a different mode to get through what was coming. Michael trusted in me and me in Source. It was a good plan.

A special bond forms when a parent cares for a child in extreme conditions. It's different, sacred, and challenging to explain. I knew that I would do anything, absolutely anything, in my power to make everything okay for my son.

Only a parent who has lived it knows what it is like to move into a hospital room in an oncology ward with crying babies all night, the overwhelming smell of urine, metal carts up and down the halls, beepers forever going off at all hours, while sleeping in a chair and waking up with every sound your child makes. The testing and poking and the much-dreaded blood draws--and the waiting.

If you're one of those parents, my heart goes out to you. If you know one of those parents, please consider getting them a coffee, making a meal, offering a hand, a hug, and a non-judgmental ear to listen with your full attention.

Angels

During all of our hospital stays, Angels were always present. I found it very odd when one would appear so clearly to me and everyone passing by not noticing its presence. Occasionally I'd witness the smile from someone who did see them. Sort of a quiet club of Angel knowers, or were they Angels too? It makes me smile thinking that. Strangers appearing out of nowhere in the precise moment they're needed, and then gone before you can thank them properly.

The Angels carried me time and time again. A ten-hour surgery was scheduled to happen a few weeks after the initial shunt surgery. The skilled surgeon was a good man. Opening Michael's skull and exposing his brain in order to retrieve an egg-sized tumor from his cerebellum was a challenging surgery. The tumor had an arm as it grew. It wrapped itself around Michael's brain stem.

I asked the surgeon how he'd know if it was the tumor and not Michael's brain tissue. Was it a different color? Did it stand out? Apparently, it's the same color as the surrounding tissue. I let him know that Michael's quality of life is more important than quantity. Parents are put in a position of making decisions for their children's lives. We do the best we can. For Michael, this was the right decision.

 It was November, the longest day of my life. Prayers were being said around the world for Michael and the surgery team. It was ten long hours in the waiting room. Friends stopped by to support us, including his amazing teacher, school friends and parents. They were always so kind and supportive. We loved them and were so grateful.

 The child psychologist assigned to Michael was present off and on, as was the head of pediatric oncology, Dr. Finklestein. It was apparent he really cared about these kids. We were blessed to have Michael's team, a group of brilliant, devoted people who became fond of him.

 That day, my prayer was like a running chant in my head. Sitting in the waiting room, I continually looked at the clock. After several hours, I got out of the chair I'd been anchored to and had oddest sensation.

I sensed the love coming to us. It felt as if the prayers and Angels were surrounding us and holding us in a bubble. I felt so light. Walking across the floor, I had the impression I was floating. I was moving but couldn't feel the floor below my feet. I consciously tried stepping harder on the floor and it didn't work. The Angels were carrying me. They were also with Michael, carrying him and the surgical team.

After hours of waiting, the surgeon came to us. Michael had made it! His head was completely wrapped with gauze and bandages.

On waking with moans, his speech was slurred, yet he was still able to form thoughts. The surgeon preformed simple neurological tests. "Touch your finger to your nose." Michael's arm went beyond his face not finding it or his nose. His legs couldn't decide if they wanted to turn when touched with a pin-type instrument. Besides recovery from having the back of his skull opened and brain manipulated, he was going to need lots of therapies. The best part was that Michael was still Michael.

When Dr. Spzer, his surgeon, unwrapped Michael's head from bandages, the opening was from the top of his head and down his neck. Blood began to drain out between the surgical staples. I grabbed gauze without thinking and mopped up the blood. The doctor looked at me with an acknowledgment that he knew I would do whatever Michael needed.

Michael had become popular because of his comprehensive communication skills. He discussed the tumor and surgeries with the doctors beforehand. They would bring in other doctors to show his abilities. Michael thought it was funny.

The oncologist was thrilled to see that Michael was doing okay after such a long surgery.

"You must be hungry," he said. "You can have anything you want. Do you want ice cream?"

"Brown rice and broccoli, please, Mom," Michael mumbled. The doctor laughed and couldn't believe his request. I was beyond delighted that Michael was still Michael!

We got to know other children the same age during our hospital stays, therapies and the yearly cancer run. There were too many children with these same tumors. After surgeries they were not always the same person.

We witnessed families breaking up in all the stress; one mother losing her mental abilities trying to cope with it all. It was disheartening to see who would make it through and who did not, who would retain the same thought skills they once had, and who would not. These young warriors were experiencing scary things, the horrific unknown. Why? What was happening to cause this? My heart goes out to each of their stories, their parents, and families. I cannot imagine being the therapist, oncologist and surgeons living with all they were seeing day in and out. May they all be blessed forever. Thank you, all.

Michael was with us and able to speak. Slurred

or not, he was thinking and expressing his needs. There was still the lingering arm of the tumor entwined with his brain stem and that was okay, for today.

The Angels were there again in recovery. They had not left. It had been the longest day with the greatest ending. We were so grateful to have Michael with us. The Angels were holding us the entire time. Is there a word beyond grateful? The Angels continued to hold us for the following hours, days, weeks, and months moving into years.

Eventually, being held by the Angels became second nature in all that happened around Michael Although never taken for granted. The ease they shared was familiar to my body, mind, spirit, and my Soul knew them. I don't know how I would have been able to be there for Michael without them. There was always something happening to Michael and they were always there for whatever it was.

After the first six years of the Angel warnings,

although grateful, there came a point of frustration that they appeared only in the toughest of times. Out of exhaustion, tired of pushing through trying times or angry, I yelled out one day. I was home alone standing in the kitchen. I was saying a prayer of thanks and it became a much-needed release of things going on. It ended with me looking up, arms held straight out, as if reaching out to them.

"Why do I only see you in the worst of times?" I cried, tears streaming down my face searching for an answer and letting them see my frustration.

" I want you in my life every day! If you don't want to be here every day, then don't come when something is about to happen! I need you all of the time!" The tears kept coming. How could I make demands upon the Angels and GOD? I needed to express my feelings.

Love made it safe to do, so I did. Faith in their love gave me the permission to know it was okay for me to yell at the Angels. It gave me the strength to say what I needed without fear of judgement. The Angels were not going to think of me as ungrateful. In that moment, I felt them come around me, hugging and touching me. In the past when I felt their presence and the feeling of being carried, it was off my body. It was a sense of their nearness and warmth. Now, the physical sensation of touching was to a greater degree. Their steadfast presence, like no other, was right there with me. It wasn't a warning this time or a message saying everything will be okay. This was so different. They directly responded to my need for them. Had they been waiting for my permission? If so, I gave it— that day and every day since.

"Angels of Light that are only for my greatest and highest good, touch me now, hold me in this day, and everyday forward."

A prayer of intention that has held me up when I felt I could take no more. A prayer of joy and gratitude seeing new grass in spring, baby ducks swimming on the river, a child's giggle...all of these things. Every time I smile or laugh, I want to share that with the Angels. I wanted them with me all the time, not just in bad times, I shared all the wonderful things with them too!

I've never witnessed an angry, jealous, or selfish Angel. When more than one is present, whatever is needed is done with grace and love. There's a beauty in watching what happens when a team of them is present for healing. An ease in all movements and warmth, with no hesitation. Moving with a knowing, all connected into the same thought and intention, always with Love. Angels listen to all conversations, know our thoughts, and see everything we do. Yes, even watching me write this and you reading it. They guide us to healing and deeper understandings.

They know our Souls, which is everything about us. Angels also have a sense of humor and playfulness. Babies giggle when no one is around. Who do you think they're talking to? Over the years, they've smiled at me while I question them. How hilarious I am to question an Angel, but I do, knowing it's okay. They are the most patient Beings/Energies. They delight in my joys and hold me when I need holding. When I am about to make a bad choice, they don't say a word. Instead, they watch to see what I choose. They are here to support and guide, not decide for us.

The Angels presence was affirmed daily. One cool, rainy day in February, I was driving on a slick highway near Pomona, California. I was singing along with the radio, when suddenly, a few car lengths in front of me, a car started spinning. It was in the lane next to me. I slowed down, along with several other cars. The challenge was slowing down fast enough so as to not hit the other car. It stopped spinning, but my heart kept pounding as the car was now facing me and traveling toward me. My car hadn't come to a complete halt yet, either. The driver of the other vehicle, a woman, locked eyes with me as we watched our cars inch closer together. Were our thoughts the same? This was it? We were going to crash head on into each other.

All at once, both cars came to a halt. I could feel the Angels present. We did not get out of our cars. We didn't need to. When our vehicles touched, it was more of a kiss than a bump. Traffic had paused with the exception of a few impatient drivers going around us. We looked at each other wide-eyed through the wet windshield, knowing that this was a gift. I thanked the Angels. I wondered what she was thinking. The woman reversed her car, turned around, moved to the side of the road, and sat. Most likely to gather her thoughts. Maybe to say thank you. Since there was no accident or damage, I continued on in gratitude. Thank you, Angels!

Things like that happened on a regular basis. I am grateful every time, in all things. Angels are there when times are difficult as well as in all of the little things. What gifts they are every day. Why people don't acknowledge connect with them amazes me. Of course, we each have free will and choose our own journey. I choose Angels!

LOVE

I wish you could've known Michael before the tumor. Here's a little bit of what he was like.

When he was five years old, we had family meetings to discuss things happening in our lives. When something needed to be said, we'd gather around the long, oak dining room table.

On one occasion when Michael called the meeting, he seemed profoundly serious. It was cute. Giving him the respect due, I sat quietly and listened.
"I don't want to be treated like a kid anymore," he said. "I want to be treated like an adult."

He was dead serious. He wasn't angry, just wanted to get things clear with us. This kiddo was beyond his years and extraordinary. He wanted to be talked to like an adult. We each took turns sharing and agreed on terms that suited everyone. With a look of satisfaction at what he'd accomplished, I thought about how cool he was to be able to call a meeting and say what he needed to say. That's the kind of person Michael was at five.

In between everything happening to him physically, we had exceptional times. Life becomes clearer when you know how short it can be. Every day is appreciated and celebrated.

The portion of the tumor that remained on his brain became a part of the holidays with its own Christmas stocking: an old beaten-up white sock with a hole. The word Tumor was written in black marker down the length of it. It stood out next to the cross-stitched ones I'd made for everyone else. Santa would fill it with vitamin C tablets. Something healthy to help it go away!

When Michael was studying dinosaurs, we made the tumor out of play dough and his plastic dinosaurs would come and stomp on it and eat it. It was annihilated over and over. It was great to play and giggle, but at one point, Michael felt bad for the tumor. I explained that it didn't belong in his body and we were encouraging it to leave. He was okay with that and continued on in a variety of ways to bring it to its demise.

We would sing in the hot tub. He created this little ditty:
>Hurray for me!
>(Wet raspberry sound) to the tumor!
>(Wet raspberry sound), to the tumor!
>(Wet raspberry sound), to the tumor!
>La la la la la...

We'd all laugh and make raspberry sounds. How many tumors are sung to? Michael's was.

There was another bump in the road when Michael was nine. A tumor had grown on his spine that would require surgery to remove it. This could have been a remnant from the ten-hour tumor removal surgery he had when he was five Blood could have dripped down and formed this new tumor mass. No one really knew the answer.

The delicate surgery on his spine went well. He came out of it needing physical therapy to walk. He was sent home to recover after a week at the hospital, where we knew he'd have a quicker recovery.

Within a month, he was swimming laps in the pool as part of his recovery program. After years of therapies to regain abilities, this one was not going well. Let's face it, no one enjoys physical therapy. It's hard work and hurts. His body and mind were getting tired of having to go through this process again and again.

He was so unhappy performing his rehab tasks, complaining of pain. He started to show other signs, too. Something wasn't right.

We went to the hospital for a CT scan. As I sat waiting in the hallway of hospital basement, I could feel the presence of the Angels, so I knew something was up.

The same assurance I'd received four years earlier while watching television came to me.

"All will be okay," I heard in my heart and mind, assuring me once again to trust.

A thick cinder block wall separated me from my son while he was getting the scan. To my surprise, the Angels gave me a view opened through the wall, as if the Angels had erased an opening so I could see Michael lying on the table with the CT machine over him. This was a first. I didn't understand how or why, I just trusted.

The tumor that had been removed was back. It had grown in the same place on his spine. He was going into surgery soon after the scan. It all happened so quickly. After hours of waiting during surgery, I was finally able to see him.

There was a nurse in his room as he slept.
"Your son is a paraplegic," she said as I stood by his bed.
She came over and touched my arm, maybe to ground me or make sure I was conscious of what she had just said.
Perhaps thinking I didn't hear her, she repeated herself.
"Michael is a paraplegic."

I looked her in the eyes to let her know I'd heard her.

"Okay," I said. "Teach me what I need to know."

She didn't understand that I was just so happy he was alive and breathing. She didn't understand what the Angels had told me earlier: "All will be okay." I believed that with all my heart.

So many trials of strength, patience, and constant fatigue come with a child with a brain tumor. You pull out all the stops for your child who has lost all feeling from the hips down. I'll never know what it's like for him to no longer have the ability to walk, run, or even go to the bathroom.

We didn't have extra help and his care was 99percent on my shoulders. There were times he'd be so mean after surgeries. I'd leave his room, go to my bedroom, sit on the floor and sob. I knew he didn't mean it, but it was like being beaten up. After a good, efficient cry, I'd wash my face and go back to him. To say it was difficult is putting it mildly. There wasn't another option but to go on. It wasn't his fault, that was clear. He was always doing the best he could.

We spent the rest of his third-grade homeschooling. It was huge adjusting to a wheelchair and all that it involves. The schooling part was the lesser challenge. He loved learning, but the wheelchair was a block from the life he knew. We created a "new normal" with new ways to deal with the demands that come with a paraplegic.

Unexperienced in the beginning, it took extreme efforts to adapt to this lifestyle. It took four hours to get up, eat, use the bathroom, shower, and get dressed. And that's after we had the procedures down pat. Everything in the house needs to be moved or adjusted. Meanwhile, staying firm that he become independent in order that he lived life to the fullest. Little things were big accomplishments, and they were celebrated.

In fourth grade, Michael joined a public school. At that time, the schools weren't so accommodating for people in wheelchairs. Change was in the works, though, and we played a part in helping move things along.

The new friends Michael made were sweet and wonderful. They saw beyond his chair, beyond his differences.

These kids didn't know why Michael's hands and feet were smaller, or that his pituitary gland was affected by the tumor, or how difficult it was for him to write and how much focus he needed to do so. it took. They just saw that his writing was large and less structured than their own. They didn't understand what it was like trying so hard to fit in when the boundaries of a wheelchair hold you outside normal fourth grade activities. He was on the sidelines most of the time.

His new friends didn't share a past with him. They didn't know what he had been like before the tumor. They were seeing Michael as he was now. The ones that accepted him found a friend for life. He had big shoulders to hold a friend up when they needed support. With kindness and his huge heart, he'd listened with full attention to others' heartaches and stories. He was a great listener and didn't judge., Sometimes he'd give wise advice. He was also playful and thoughtful to the highest degree.

An annual "Wheelchair Family Olympics" was held every summer, including families from out of town. We planned different tasks and relays, with everyone taking a turn against Michael in the extra wheelchair we had. It was fun and exciting, always ending with lots of cheers and laughter.

Planning the activities for the two-day affair each year was an event. Family meetings around the table, decisions on what competitions to include, and how they would be performed. It brought so much joy to everyone involved, especially Michael.

It also was a great teaching tool for all of us. For example, one year after an event, Michael's older cousin by a handful of years, stood up from the wheelchair with ease. He looked over at Michael realizing he didn't have that same option. I saw

Jacob's beautiful, big heart affected that day. Michael was a teacher.

Being in a wheelchair all day while your body goes through growth spurts can cause issues. Michael had decided on a sportier chair, but it had less back support. This caused his back to curve quickly. After consulting a specialist and because of the extent of the curve, the decision was made to fuse his entire back.

Young as he was and from the very beginning, every surgery was always fully discussed with Michael. He had control over whether he would do it or not. I felt he needed power over this. He would take a few hours or a couple of days and then agree. This time he was not looking forward to it at all. He would be in a two-part body cast afterwards for an extended period. He'd be out of school and it meant more pain.

The spinal fusion went well. An amazing doctor flew in from Boston. He had a great spirit and understood we called in Angels to work with him. He welcomed them.

Titanium rods were placed on either side of Michael's spine with wires attached and clipped onto the bone. Growth plates were removed during this process. Michael would no longer be able to bend at the waste or have MRI scans. On the bright side, he gained three plus inches in height from the surgery! He was happy he outgrew another wheelchair and could now see better over the sink to look in the mirror while he brushed his teeth.

One afternoon during Michael's recovery at home, I put him in his body cast that encompassed his entire torso, out of his wheelchair and into bed so he could rest while I made dinner.

His brother, Nathan, was in the family room playing a video game. My husband came in the house to take a break from yard work. We were chatting when suddenly Nathan said, "I smell smoke!"
"Must be my cooking," I said, making a joke.
It got stronger. Nathan ran to the front door to see where it was coming from.

"Fire!" he yelled at the top of his lungs.

Flames poured from the garage door. Plastic toys hanging from the garage ceiling were melting.

A stranger our garden hose and tried to contain the fire. Black smoke filled the air.

"Call 911!" I yelled. "Nathan, go to the sidewalk where you'll be safe!"

"Get the dogs out back!" I told my husband. "I'll go get Michael!"

Michael was sleeping. "Wake up," I said as I grabbed his body armor. "We have to move fast."

My mind raced. In the garage, I had a kiln, ceramic supplies, materials for screen printing—inks, solutions, and chemicals. Due to their proximity with the boys' bedroom, if anything exploded, Michael and I could end up stuck in his room with no way out.

The only way he could leave was in his wheelchair, with the body form supporting his spine.

Getting the form on he had to be rolled from side to side gently, strapping the front and back together, before lifting him out of bed. His back was still tender with the surgery opening still healing down his entire back. There was also the fact that his legs would flop. It typically took about thirty minutes to do this.

Trying to remain calm, yet clear, I explained the urgency of the situation to Michael. That's when the Angels came. My hands began to do what needed to be done.

"The Angels are here helping us," I said.

Amazingly, the Angels were actually helping maneuver my son. It was usually a bit of a struggle for me to lift Michael and put him on his transfer board in order to slide him into his wheelchair. With the Angels help, Michael felt as light as a feather. It wasn't me doing this, it was the Angels!

By the time we got to the safety of the front door, the fire department had arrived. They were hosing down the garage.

Everything in the garage was damaged. Remnants of what was once bright colored plastic children's toys were now blackened and dripped down from the rafters, where they'd been stored. My creative outlets of printing and ceramics were gone. The contents of the attic were all smoke damaged, including Christmas decorations and my wedding dress. We were all safe, though, and that's all that mattered.

That stranger who grabbed the garden hose was gone. None of the neighbors gathered knew who he was. Nathan had never seen him before. Maybe he was an Angel. My instinct says he was. I believe there's an Angel inside each of us.

Apparently, the cause of the fire involved a plugged-in extension cord outside of the garage. The firemen were amazing—thoughtful, kind, and efficient. Afterward, they took the time to talk with us, helping us relax and look at the situation. They suggested we stay somewhere else for the night, in case the fire flared up again, but with Michael's back care, I felt better staying home. I monitored the situation by staying awake all night and writing Christmas cards.

By age fourteen, 1994, Michael's hearing began to decrease rapidly. Hearing loss was happening in the other children who had also received radiation treatments. It was an unexpected residual effect from it, which, at age six, Michael was given treatments twice a day for three months, except weekends and holidays. That always made me wonder: Tumors don't grow on weekends and holidays?

Our family began taking sign language classes. Michael left public high school and went to a deaf school that was hours away. He was up at 4:00 AM in the morning to catch a bus and didn't return home until close to 5:00 PM every afternoon. For the first time in his life, he hated school.

Months passed, a family meeting was called, and

it was decided he'd return to his old school. He figured if he was going to be living in a hearing world, he may as well get used to it and be with his friends.

As a boy, Michael would take my hand and hold it for no reason. When he started school, I was ready for this to end, understanding he wouldn't want to be embarrassed in front of friends. That never happened. When other little boys were dropping their mom's hands, he continued to hold mine until we said goodbye.

Even in front of friends in high school he'd take my hand. To him, it didn't matter what anyone thought about it.

Michael's sensitivity towards me and others was one of an old Soul from the beginning. He was like an adult man talking to me, with his arm resting on mine or holding my hand. Regardless of who he was talking to, friends, family, or strangers, he gave his full attention, looking the person right in the eye. He was present, even if he was dealing with his own health issues.

I assumed Michael's communications skills were normal, until someone informed me that most kids aren't putting sentences together at 18 months. He learned to read at an early age, too. He quickly memorized everything that was read to him and if you skipped a word, he'd make you stop, and reread the page. His grandfather got a kick out of that.

The books grew thicker and still he knew every word. He caught on to reading between three and four, and never stopped. By five he was reading, *The Chronicles of Narnia*. He'd also expanded his math skills.

To keep him excited about math, I'd go into his bedroom as he slept and to draw out a simple algebra story problem on the black board. He'd run out of his room, stopping at the end of the hall and give a victory yell. " Yes!" It warmed my heart.

He loved reading. Not just liked reading, loved it.

Everything about dinosaurs was devoured. We all took an enriching summer to study them when he was six and Nathan was two. We explored the dinosaur's movements from the tarpits in Los Angeles, a family favorite, across the states and ending at the great museum in Denver.

Michael discovered many authors. J.J.R.Tolkien was his all-time favorite and he read it every year from grade three on. It was a place he could go in his mind away from everything happening in his life and be a part of the adventure. His mind loved adventures.

When J.K.Rowling's Harry Potter series came on the scene, he was in heaven. It was also a way he connected with other people around the world on blogs and chats. So many were passionate about her stories. We always had to be at the bookstore, even in the middle of the night, to buy the new release. He disappeared and read around the clock until he announced that he was finished reading the book. He'd look worn out but joyful and satisfied of gaining another story level. His books were like another set of constant friends.

He dreamed of living on his own and accomplished that. He dreamed of traveling and with the help of his cousin Susie, he did.

He had many health issues throughout the years went. Decubitus Ulcers, pressure sores--they're a threat to everyone in wheelchairs. Skin breakdown is a part of life. It began in high school and the older he got, the worse it all became. There were surgeries to replace tissue from one place to another. His lower body began to look like a jigsaw puzzle.

Michael had extended stays in nursing homes when it was more than simple wound care I could deal with. At one point, he spent 10 months in a Clinitron bed, unable to get out of it. It looked like a big metal elongated bathtub that Michael was hoisted into. Under the thin flowing cover, sand is kept moving by fans. This relieves pressure to the skin that caused the ulcer to begin with. The fan was loud and constant. He had a bar above him to pull himself up to move, shifting side to side or to his back, his only three positions.

A wound vacuum patch was placed over the dinner plate size ulcer that had broken down on his lower back and butt to the bone. The suction of the vacuum kept pulling blood up out of him to encourage new tissue growth to fill in the massive hole in his back. That lasted 10 months. To live through that, he relied on his amazing inner strength.

MRSA happened during a hospital stay requiring another surgery to remove tail bone that had become infected by it. He faced it all only as Michael could.

Along the way he made friends of all ages. He enjoyed the senior crowd his entire life. As a child he chose adults over children. He liked hearing what they knew and the interaction in the discussions.

Michael's dream was to become a teacher. He was disappointed when he realized it wasn't going to happen. His body wouldn't allow it. I told him that he had always been a teacher. That he was a teacher to me and all those around him. He was a teacher to all who didn't understand different or wheelchairs. He took that, held onto it, and became a tutor to other students

It wasn't Michael's way to put blame on others for what was happening to him. He understood forgiveness and how important it is. The focus was to continue on, going forward. Sure, there was anger at times and that is why I was the advocate, protector, and lioness for him. He had enough to deal with. His job was healing and going forward. Everyone needs an educated advocate. Please make certain your loved ones have one in you.

Michael had a mental list of things he wanted to accomplish, which he shared with me many times. As he was checking them off, I wondered what he would do when they were all completed. Looking back at it now, I see that he knew that when the list was done… he could leave

Trauma

The first time I held nephew I was twelve years old. In July, 1969, Scotty was the first grandchild and my first nephew. This sweet baby boy opened my nurturing heart from day one. I got to hold a baby! He came in healing so much for everyone around him.

Seven years prior my mother at thirty eight years old, lost her final baby on Oct 2, 1962. Thomas was full term and due to circumstances at the hospital strangled at birth with the chord wrapped around his neck. My mother was alone in a small room because there was no room in delivery. She called it a broom closet. I can not image what that was like for her. It breaks my heart thinking of it now.

I witnessed her grief as she shut down from being the caring mother I had known for the first five years of my life. My young mind didn't understand her choices or any of it. In those days things like this were not spoken of openly, at least not in our household. I was left alone grieving not only the loss of a baby, my brother, that I longed to hold, I grieved the loss of my mother being fully present.

I missed my hand feeling the baby kick in her tummy and having her read books to me. I missed her smile. I did not understand the changes happening. The baby clothes promised to me, for my dolls, that we had ironed and put in the drawers together, were taken out and burned. Life in the house was more like a tomb seeming robotic. Everyone moved on keeping their pain to themselves, pushing it down. This changes lives, it changed mine. I quieted and shut down.

Loss as a child finds a place not only in the heart but in the mind forming decisions until healing occurs. If grieving had been acknowledged and nurtured life may have been softer, it wasn't.

It was July of 1969, my oldest brother back from Vietnam fathered a son. That first grand child, Scotty, being born was helping ease the wounds in my mother's heart and mine. His presence cemented my great desire to one day be a mother. In my heart I knew I was suppose to have wonderful babies, like this one. I would love my children with all of my heart. I would not shut down. These things I already had learned at five. Lessons come in all experiences.

Sadly the story of Scotty's childhood is not a kind one. The challenges he faced on earth were of abuse and loneliness in the secrets of protecting his abusers. He took these traumas in and buried his pain as any unsupported child does. We both understood shutting down and hiding pain unable to communicate it or be heard.

We were very close, sharing a bond that neither of us fully understood. He and I embraced the comfort, trust and love we had in each other. Our wounded child knew the other, both of us imprinted by a human or experience.

Scott grew up holding secrets that were eating him up from within. He was a married man and had his own baby when he began therapy to heal his past.

Only then he came to visit me and shared his full story. With great courage he was determined to heal.

He drove down from Vegas with his family. We went for a walk to have time alone from everyone. He asked and I was sharing with him the medical issues Michael was dealing with in high school.

We began to talk about secrets. I shared how they protect predators. It confuses you as a child. It shakes and distorts what real love is. It dismantles you. Who can you trust? You end up accepting abuse because it becomes a part of what you believe to be love. You learn to accept abuse from people who say they love you, or are supposed to love you, because of that dark imprint.

Abuse is not love. Until you begin healing and learn deep within what that truth is, you will be faced with abusers. Once learning the truth, your radar will spot an abuser and you can make the choice to stand up for yourself. This luxury isn't available to a young child or baby.

I know this because I also lived it. It took years for me to clear that imprint from my heart, mind, Spirit, and body. Today I am strong in the understanding of what love is. As an adult, Scotty was determined to be free from his imprint.

After sharing what I knew Scott began to bring up memories. He filled in the blanks with his truth and shared in detail what happened, this person was suppose to have loved and protect him, he did not. We cried and held hands as he talked about dealing with years of abuse and the struggle protecting his maternal grandfather. I felt sick to my stomach, my heart breaking for all he had endured.

The abuse had been what broke his amazing little boy spirit, not his parents divorce, as we had thought. My family saw the change at before 3 years of age and never put the pieces together. During the visit, I saw how strong his spirit is to reach out from the trauma and take back his life.

I wish all children could know that the predator cares nothing about their needs, it is all about them. Holding their secrets takes away your power. A child quiets in powerlessness. With love, conscious support and healing the traumatized child in all of us can move beyond the pain. It is our choice to make, in our timing. We are survivors, that is what we do. I wish we would all thrive in this life instead of just survive.

Scott is a wonderful example of healing. He was determined to be free from his childhood imprint. He was learning love through his children and wife. They gave him the confidence to choose freedom from the past.

The following year, 2000, Scotty was on his motorcycle on a mountain road in California with friends. He drove off, separating from the group and disappeared over the edge of the cliff. Was it an animal on the road? His motorcycle had fallen on its side and skidded a long distance pinning him under it. A hole was worn in the side of his helmet before going over. He was 33.

I like to think that his last thoughts were of his wife, son and baby girl, Hailey. He is fully free from the childhood traumas.

Scotty did learn what real love was in his lifetime and that will never end. He was the great dad he wanted to be. I believe his love continues as he watches over his family and he will never be forgotten, ever. I could not write my heart story without including the one Soul that began the nurturing heart in me, Thomas, my baby brother, or the one who opened it, Scott. I Love you both forever.

Trauma effects us all differently. Michael went through so many traumas in his life. He didn't have to get quiet or loose his spirit, I supported him everyday. He did not see himself as a victim. Scott chose not to be a victim. It is an energy imprint we slip into forming a life of its own. I am a work in progress healing that within me.

Choosing to Heal

I happened to be able to function in hospital and caregiving situations, my husband did not. The illusion we had portrayed as our life as a couple was crumbling. He worked and I cared for the boys, house and him. I was feeling over whelmed. It took a toll on an already fractured relationship.

It was 1999 and I left the state with the intention of divorce immediately, I was done. The boys I can only imagine were in shock by my quick exit. They didn't know the inner workings of our marriage and how unhealthy it was for me.

Nathan at sixteen only saw the world he had known crumbling. Michael without hesitation, joined me in Michigan within the month as I settled in. Nathan chose to remain in California. He reacted and was not supported enough to heal his wounds. In his pain he made a decision that I was no longer his mother.

He may not have had much control in his life. He made certain he controlled our relationship. Bit by bit he created a barrier allowing me a smaller and smaller place in his life. I was not prefect, I am not claiming that. In our separation we did the best we could with that tools we had at the time.

Before the end of 2002 I was remarried and supporting Michael living 10 miles away. He lived independently yet, close enough for me to be on call, if he needed assistance. I was his back up and a hug not far away. There were many times over the next 12 years that I was called on around the clock for help. We had a system that worked. He was a grown man needing his space. He loved the ability to have his own life of independence.

Our bodies, our wonderful bodies, take on our traumas. Sometimes it's stored in the mind, sometimes in a part of the body.

After ten years of marriage my husband began a life style journey that put an end our union. It was a shock that struck me to my core. My world, as I knew it, collapsed and the person who I thought was my best friend, was not. My body didn't know what to do with the pain and it ended up collecting in my gallbladder.

There were no warning signs that I could remember. The pain came in the middle of the night and was intense. I had no idea what it was. I called 911 and crawled to the front door, unlocking it before I began throwing up on the wood floor near the door. I heard the siren and was on the gurney heading to the hospital. It was scary having no one at home to meet me.

To be alone in this was an experience was something I never thought would happen and yet it was. Michael always had me to support him during all the years of emergencies, ambulance rides because of seizures, and so many other issues. He always had me nearby to say, "I love you." And here I was alone, no one to hold my hand.

In the emergency room after tests were run, I was

given pain relief while I waited. It was clearly my gallbladder. Two nurses came in separately and looked at the film up on the lit screen. It was the first time seeing inside my own body. It had always been Michael's brain, spine, gallbladder, and kidneys.

Mine was filled with a dense foggy ghost shape, large and still. Not stones like Michael had in his kidney. Both nurses said that it's emotional. One asked what I was going through. She made a sound and acknowledged that divorce is heartbreaking.

The gallbladder would have to be removed. Then, it was decided that I needed more test run because there was a concern that it was stomach cancer because of my sudden weight loss. I knew in my heart and with guidance from the Angels that this was not in my stomach, but doctors weren't going to listen to me.

It was close to the holidays and to my shock and dismay, I was sent home. The instructions were to go for testing after the holidays and sometime in January, it would be removed. Meanwhile, I was told for the next attack to come back to emergency. What! I explained that I lived alone and that I was afraid to have another attack. It didn't matter and home I went. I couldn't believe I was released.

All of those years of being an advocate for Michael turned me into a lioness over and over to get the care he needed. Where was mine? Being a self- advocate when you are scared and alone is tough. We aren't taught this. The skills from many years with Michael were now turned towards me. Instead of
calling doctor offices for my son, it was for me.

It took a series of calls trying to make doctors and scheduling fully understand what I needed. I know my strength was coming from beyond me and I am grateful for that. A date was finally set. A close friend was going to be there with me. What a huge relief to have an Angel in the waiting room.

She sat with me while I prepped for the outpatient surgery. We were close and I had shared many stories with her of Michael over the years. She was going to call him when I came out of surgery and answer any of his questions. She is a good friend. Thank you, Sue.

Before each of Michael's numerous surgeries, I always kissed him on his forehead right before he went in. It wasn't a goodbye, more of a "I'll be right here waiting." Sue and I said a prayer together, me thanking my gallbladder for taking on my pain, asking the Angels to watch over all of the nurses and doctor, and all caregivers who would be caring for me.

When it was time to wheel me out for surgery from the waiting area, my friend, remembering my stories and how alone I felt, kissed me on my forehead. I cry now feeling what a kind gesture that was. My life was filled with unkindness at that point and my heart needed this kindness. Did Sue know what peace she brought to me? I hope so and hope everyone is blessed enough to have a friend like this.

Before surgery began, I told the doctor that I was asking the Angels to guide his hands. It's always a risk to say anything about Angels because of the reaction from others. I've gone through years of that and I am so over being concerned of others judgment of me. So, I asked if that was okay. He smiled and said yes. If he believed or not, it didn't matter. When I asked him to accept it, the room filled with Angels. I knew they would be there for me, all present.

Sue relayed to me what went on in the waiting room, when she was allowed to come back to see me in recovery. The doctor found her out in the waiting room sitting with dozens of other people. He immediately said that I was doing good and all went well. Then he sat down next to her. She said, "He asked what you did." She told him that I worked with Angels. He said he believed her. The surgery was scheduled to take much longer than it took to perform. He shared with her that he felt something.

The Angels never let you down. Life may come at you and shift an outcome you want, but they never let you down, ever. All they need is you to give permission. I'm always telling people, "Give permission for your Angels to touch you and they will." Try it!

My friend and I smiled after she retold the story about the doctor's questions. Sue was used to this sort of thing happening around me. She has Angels around her too. We all do. It may feel silly to trust that it's true or that's it's out of someone's comfort zone, and that is okay.

Sometimes Angels are silent, sometimes they twiddle their thumbs patiently waiting to be acknowledged. Babies and small children see them. Life tends to cloud the way and then many times they are forgotten. They don't leave, instead they're more to the side because this is your journey and you have free will. My choice was to move forward with them by my side. It's all choice.

Learning from all that happens to us and around us is so important. These occurrences in our lives prepare us to go on. If we grow through a challenge, we gain strength. That's my conscious goal—to gain knowledge and move on with that knowledge to guide me forward. I think people forget that we are here for our Souls to grow through life experiences.

Growth is not always happy or easy. It can be gut wrenching pain and heartache. The most growth comes in how we move through it and what we take from it.

Our hearts and how we love are advance classes in growth. To put our heart out there, to take a chance to love others, to love our children and grandchildren is our greatest gift. With some we receive an innocent love in return and that's warming, peaceful, calming and makes your heart glow. To not have our love reciprocated may feel vacant. That's okay, some people have a larger capacity to love. Loving is a muscle. The more you love the stronger it gets. Mine is worked out daily. How about yours?

In 2000, therapy workshops opened up to me. In the workshops I was drawn to healing emotional and physical traumas. That led me into a new world of study. For years I'd experienced healing circles, healing modalities, learning then teaching them. Training for highest level of Reiki healing was a normal progression. The 2000's were all about hands-on healing, group gatherings, and awesome experiences.

The relief and pure joy that came when someone would release a trauma was beautiful. We all healed and grew together. Being able to see the Angels was always helpful. Many don't and they work on trust, which says so much for them. Their experience here is apparently about learning trust and they are. It was an amazing decade to be in.

Angels seemed ready to appear everywhere. People began talking even more openly about their own experiences without concern for judgment. Thank you to all those who spoke up before us to open the door and pave the way so we could have these wonderful experiences and not hide them.

Watching, witnessing, and assisting in years of working with others grow and heal was the best time to learn. There were friendships, community, and progress in growth. The warriors stepped up and opened their hearts to free themselves of what life does to a Spirit, Mind, Body and Soul. The stories are numerous, and I treasure each one. I'm so humbled and honored to have been a part of any of it, on any level.

Changes began happening in the spiritual community around 2011. It was like watching Brigadoon's fog come back up over a village to disappear into a time fog. In the story of Brigadoon, a classic movie with Gene Kelly, there's a small village with a bridge. Once every hundred years, the village bridge appears to outsiders for a day, and then fades back into a time, out of time. That's what it felt like for me by 2012. The door, or bridge, was fogging over. It was all changing. The Angels were giving us more space.

The time/phase we had just been in was fading. Groups of people that had gathered were ending. It was a time to go within is what I heard over and over from the Angels. It was time for everyone to make their own inner connection, instead of having others see for them or guide them. That's when I became more quiet.

My own health issue, still a challenge, is RSD, Reflex sympathetic dystrophy. Every day I feel pain. Nerve pain is sharp, throbbing, somedays I do not function well. The challenge is to think clearly and be present for others. Somedays I succeed and others I stay home. People don't see always RSD, so they don't know to offer help. I used to tease, "I'm a healer, but apparently not of this." I'm still working on it!

We can become victims of what is directed towards us and to us. There is an energy held in that word. If we take it on, it seems to include us with vast number of humans on the planet. It's an unconscious collective that sticks together, a heavy weight to carry. It is a burden worn as a badge on some. It doesn't make life better. It's a burden and holds you in a place of being stuck. If you choose to carry that, it's is your choice. I suggest choosing not to carry it.

When I look back at my own childhood, I was given handfuls of reasons to stay stuck as a victim. Thankfully, years of study, learning, and experiences have brought me out of victim into an understanding that those were and are experiences happening in my life and around me. I can take them on and carry them in a huge bag over my shoulder dragging them with me to my grave or I can look at each one, explore and choose.

In exploration, what is it I am to learn? Keeping the wisdom from each one and asking that the rest be released to GOD/Source/Creator. The Angels assist when our free will allows it to happen. I'm not saying I'm fully living this yet. I give it the most conscious effort each day in the moment I am in. Bits and pieces sneak up and I still react sometimes. Then I find myself laughing inside, as I've come face to face with another choice to make. Do I retain the anger or whatever emotion is attached to what it is…or do I pause? That Divine Pause allows a different choice to be made. In choosing a different choice, I am changing, growing.

The only thing that really changes is us. Others will not change their behavior until they grow and make a new choice. I've learned to move away from situations and people who are choosing to stay stuck in their need to abuse in any way. That is their story, it does not have to be mine.

Abusers may not see, or chose to see, that they are holding onto their own traumas and feeding into the victim energy. Being a victim may push them to create victims around them in order to not be alone. It may shut them down. That depends on their personality. It's all so fascinating!

My mother was a victim. She was a victim of her childhood, her marriage, and life. In her eyes, she could not see beyond that. She was taught to always put up a brave front. She was angry inside. She had a great capacity to do things different but out of fear, I feel she was stuck. As a child of this, it's challenging. She did the best she could. I can imagine her being an awesome mom if she could have healed. She did not, while on earth.

In the last few months and weeks of her life, it all became heavier and heavier on her shoulders. In secret, she wrote horrible stories in a journal she wanted us to find once she was dead. She wrote of her hurt and anger. I kept waiting, turning the pages for a message to her children; one of love and sharing a moment or some bit of tenderness showing her love for us. There was none. She left this so we would know of her pain and how she had been wronged.

Were we supposed to take on her burden and continue to carry it for her? That's a trick of family ancestry that has gone on through time. What if we don't take it on from another's experience? What if her story, sadness, heartache, burdens, fear, and hate could be let go and laid to rest with her? I wanted to just love her, not take on her "stuff."

A few weeks before she passed, I visited and found the energy in the house heavy. Her pain was hanging in the air. She was on oxygen and meds for several issues. She was miserable struggling.

It was hard for her to sit or move, and her speech was labored with pauses as she tried to catch her breath.

"Mom," I said, "Do you want me to help lighten it up in here for you? We can clear this energy out if you like. It feels so heavy in here."

"No, it's mine," she said in a voice that no longer had any lilt to it. It was raspy, drained, and low.

My heart broke for her. She did feel it all around her. She chose to hang on to it all. It owned her. In that moment, I loved my mom. I loved her because that was the only thing I could do for her.

She didn't really like to be hugged by me. I don't know if anyone else felt this, but when I hugged my mother, she would allow me in just a little bit and then the wall would appear, and I would be hugging a wall.

I grew up feeling this and had thought someday I'm going to squeeze her passed it. I'd smile inside when the wall came in each hug. I even began to think that I loved the wall, too. Heck, she was who she was. She hadn't had my experiences, only hers. From her upbringing, she was still believed that God was fire and brimstone. I do not.

Mom had a need inside her to remain as she was. The last day was sad and a blessing at the same time. The day before she passed, I witnessed something really beautiful. In those moments, through her, I learned further what happens at the time of passing. I am thankful for you, Mom. I love you.

Beyond seeing what happened between her and the Angels, we never could find a lasting sweetness in our relationship. We had moments that I treasure. Mostly, though, it was a challenge. I longed for her, as a child growing up.

I can share stories now to help show others what is

healthy and not. It isn't about making her bad. She carried burdens and didn't choose to know it any different. From stories with her, I can share with others how to not carry trauma, how to not allow those burdens to be the weights on your shoulders and cover your heart. Lessons come in all ways. She may have been my inspiration to write, beginning with that yellow legal pad in third grade, how I would parent different.

Having free will, you can choose to learn new ways! That's the beauty of this life.

People will come and go with lessons. Instead of carrying the hardships of the lessons, decide to carry only the wisdom learned in the lesson. Perhaps if you haven't learned the wisdom, the lesson will stick around or repeat until you do. It's not about you, me, or anyone being a victim. It is about our Soul's growth in every experience here. We can make an oops, we can forget, and we can get back on track and see things for what they really are and move forward. It's all in our choices.

I began making a conscious choice to be different when I was in third grade. Life wasn't as sweet as it was on TV, movies, or what I thought was going on in other households. Now I know every household had its own challenges one way or another. I was an extremely sensitive little girl, crying easily. Many times, I was told, "You're too sensitive," as if it was the worst thing I could ever be.

I had an uncle who, for some reason, needed to make me feel little. Clearly now, I see he had his own issues. Then, I didn't have that knowledge. To me, he was hurtful, and I always fell into his emotional beat-me-up traps. He'd wait until the entire family was sitting around the table and make a comment at me.

"How fast can I make her cry?"

Like it was a game and I was his prey. It happened over and over and as a small skinny little thing, I could feel the tears building up in my eyes. Everyone would remain silent.

"The tears are building up," he'd say victoriously or keep going until they ran down my cheeks.

My father, my mom, my cousins, other uncles, aunts, and brothers—they were all silent. I'd get up from the table and leave to go cry alone or be ordered to sit there.

Once my mom said, "That's enough." Not standing up and making the statement, she said like you would to a little boy poking a stick at a dead turtle. I wondered why my uncle needed to do that. I know today, as an educated adult. As a child, what I learned was to take abuse and shut up, push it down.

A child in our household, as in many in the 60's, you were to be seen and not heard, period. My viewpoint wasn't needed or wanted. Years later, it gave me great stuff to work on in healing workshops and therapies. I learned so much about myself and all involved through that. I no longer push things down.

I was a serious little girl seeing and experiencing things that I didn't feel were right. I needed to do something about it, so I asked my father to bring home a yellow legal pad from work. In my mind, it made it all so much more powerful by having a legal pad. I wrote about things that happened and how I, as a parent, would do it different. It was an outlet. I wasn't hurting anyone, and it allowed me to see things that were happening from a different perspective. I was in third grade and did the best I could.

The pages filled up over the years. I still have many vivid memories of things that happened. I see them, hear the voices, smell the smells, and can feel what it was for me then and to be back in it. I've always thought everything stayed so clear so I could learn and help others to find their way out. Memories are for a reason. I use mine to teach and to heal.

A Mother's Heart

Two years ago, my thirteen-year-old puppy, Gracie, was put to sleep. This sweet loyal companion always gave so much love. It was a heart shock saying goodbye to her gentleness and spirit.

It reminded me of the heart shock when my mother died in 2006, fourteen years before. I am not comparing my dog to my mother. Just explaining how my heart experienced each loss in different ways.

When my mom passed, a piece of my heart ached in a way that could only be for the one who gave birth to me. An entire portion of my heart that I'd been unaware of felt like it lifted from my body. No matter what our relationship was, she held a place designated only for her. It ached for the lost possibility of what we could have been; it ached for her and why she was the way she was. It ached in a way different from any other. It was very sacred.

There is my heart for Michael. Mother and child

are a unique connection. Ours was… are there words? A parent who has been caregiver and has gone through as much as Michael and I did have something beyond words. He was the first and only person that loved me without conditions. He taught me what love really is.

Michael was back in the hospital again in 2012. He was now 32 years old. In the morning, he had surgery to put in a feeding tube. I went home for a break and returned in the evening. I sat on the bottom of the bed and he held my hand, as he always did. We talked about what was happening. He was bracing himself for yet another hurdle to work through.

Michael always wanted to be helpful. I brought in my computer that evening to ask him advice. I knew it would get his mind moving forward to getting out of hospital and home.

He had a stroke a few days before and was left without the ability to swallow and keep it from going into his lungs. So, he was given a suction tube by which he was solely responsible to suck all saliva out of his mouth on his own. Talking was a bit of a challenge, but he was fine with pauses to use the suction.

His eyes lit up when I said, "I need your help." He became serious and told me he'd gladly take over that task for me. I was relieved. It was good to see him taking charge. We talked about so many subjects and people that night. It seemed we covered our lifetimes. We didn't always believe the same, but still respected each other.

There were memories shared, his muted laughter, a few sad moments, then muted laughter again. He had a sweetness in his giggle that made him childlike. Yet, his sensitivity and kindness were that of a wise old Soul. He had a vast knowledge of some subjects and we covered several of them that evening.

Past visiting hours, he was getting tired. I gave him a kiss goodbye on his forehead and off I went, planning to return the next morning. I remember

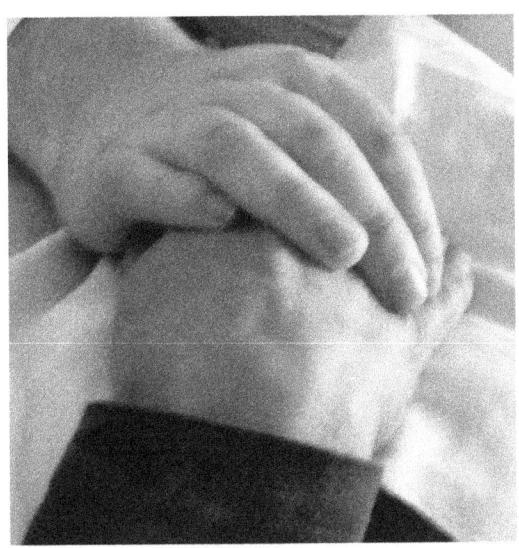

smiling and being so happy to have spent the evening with him.

The next morning as I drove back to the hospital, I decided that he wasn't going to rehab in the nursing home, as suggested by the doctor. Over the past years, he spent too many months at a time rehabbing in nursing facilities. We could handle a feeding tube at my home. I'd have a bed delivered to my living room, he'd stay with me, and we'd go about this rehab as we had before decubitus ulcers entered the picture. He'd be a part of everything and heal much faster with the TLC interaction. I was dealing with my own health issues, but I felt we could do this together.

Walking into his hospital room, things weren't right. The nurse was in attendance was busy doing things in the room. From the bottom of the bed, I called to Michael. He didn't answer.

"Oh, he's just sleeping good," the nurse said.

No, this wasn't normal. All of his life, I've looked at this person closer than most moms watching for signs and being on alert. This wasn't right.

"Michael, it's Mom," I said louder.

His color wasn't right; he was pale. I looked to the nurse. "Something is wrong. He's non responsive."

The nurse once again tried to make light of it. I cut her off and demanded a doctor, now. He appeared within a few minutes.

As he entered the room, he immediately told the nurse to get a pint of blood in him.

My heart began to ache. I knew what this was. My son was in the process of dying.

It took the nurse almost an hour to get the blood and hang it. I wanted to grab it and hook it up myself! She was young and flustered. She'd been in the room with a dying patient and didn't notice it!

A team appeared and I followed them as they wheeled Michael down the hallway. It was all blur. A nurse directed me to a waiting room. The dreaded waiting room area...I had grown to know this space so well. They're all alike with a TV on with too many seats of people waiting reading, some anxiously drinking coffee and some numb. I was in the numb group.

I knew the Angels were with us, holding Michael and me. I could feel them supporting me.

A doctor approached me. She started discussing putting my son on life support.

"NO," I blurted.

It was not in his plan. My mind flashed to conversations Michael and I had over the years. He knew his life was going to be shorter than most. We spoke openly about what he wanted. He never wanted to be hooked up to a machine. He wanted to be cremated, with his ashes taken to Ireland. We got silly about what to do with the titanium rods that were fused to his entire spine.

"Mom, make a mobile and hang crystals from it." We laughed at the thought of it.

He looked at the whole dying process differently than most. He felt all that happened to him was clearing or Karmic payback for his actions in past lives. Not everyone believes or has to believe this. He did and that's what mattered. This life, he was gentle, loving, and so forgiving. He had the kindest spirit I've ever known. His request was that we raise a glass to him and life. That was our plan and, no matter what, I was going to honor that.

"He signed a DNR!" I told the doctor.

I felt very clear about this. It was my heart talking, taking care of my baby to the end.

Again, I stated that he was not to be hooked up to life support. The doctor said it would take 15 to 20 minutes to clean him up.

"I'll give you five minutes, then I'm going in!" I could feel him slipping. My heart was speaking, aching.

A few minutes later, I walked to the room. He was still surrounded by doctors and nurses.

"Get back away from my son," I said as I entered. This wasn't about egos or medical degrees. This wasn't about them. It was about Michael and me. They quickly cleared the path. He was so still, breathing. Standing close, I saw my baby and the man he had become at the same time. I was unaware of anything else going on in the room. It was just Michael and me, as it had been his entire life. None of them knew us. They didn't know what we'd shared. My left hand went up over his heart, which was beating strong. They must have injected him with something, I thought. I can still feel the beats under my hand today. I am there with him again, in this moment. That heartbeat was our physical connection since he was in me. My heartbeat may have joined his in that moment. It felt like we were one again in this unreal happening.

My right hand began stroking the sides of his forehead, as I had always done. It calmed him before sleep as a boy. Today I was stroking his hair back away from his face, my voice in that same way as it was for my little boy. "Michael John, its Mom. I Love You. You have been the best son I could have ever asked for. You do what's best for you. Let go, sweetie. I love you. I will always love you for all time."

I continued talking to him. "Thank you, Michael, for being here. I am so grateful I got to be your mom. Let go, Michael."

Then it happened, something I had never experienced before. My left hand felt the very last beat from his big, beautiful heart. My tears fell onto him. All I knew was the Love we shared as mother and son.

The room felt as if it were filled with Light around us. A window of time or space opened for this sacred moment. I sensed my mom not far, but a bit above us. I heard her say, " Go get your boy." It was Michael's dog his grandmother was referring to.

Rosie passed a couple of years before. She was his puppy since his eighteenth birthday. That sweet girl came into the room to Michael from above him to lead the way home. He immediately went with Rosie. He left his body fully, without hesitation.

His physical body felt empty. My son was gone. Before me was the physical body I knew as him. Blood began to pour out of my sons nose as he lay there. It poured and filling his closed eye sockets. I reached for some gauze and began the task of sopping up the blood and wiping it off his face. I felt it was important that his eyes were not filled that way. A concerned nurse came over to take the gauze out of my hand.

"You don't have to do that," she said.

I calmly stopped her. "I am his mom. It's my job to do this for him."

I wiped him up as I did as a baby. Tears were everywhere on Michael, drenching my face. A calmness filled me as memories of his 32 years flashed in a matter of a few minutes. I was loving and thanking this body that held my amazing son.

Sobbing, barely able to see out of my eyes, I felt again the presence of others in the room. When I finished cleansing his face, I laid my hands on his torso.

"This man is an amazing being of Love," I said. "He is extraordinary in all ways. He is kind, thoughtful, brilliant, and a teacher to all of us. He's been a warrior. Please know who he is. He's a gift and I love him with my whole heart."

In all of the confusion, loss, and heartache, something beautiful and unexpected occurred. As my son left his body and followed his puppy away from earth, he somehow let me see through his eyes what he was seeing. It was as if the Angels opened it all up to reassure me, giving us a gift. It was so brilliant. There were vibrant colors all around Michael. Colors not found one earth. He was talking out loud to me so I could feel the experience too! "Mom, Look!" There was excitement in his voice, an exuberance and life force he hadn't had here. He was totally detached from the trauma of death. His voice was young, free, and clear. He looked back to earth and saw muted colors and expressed the difference as we viewed it together. There was such vibrance in his voice. My heart was so happy for him to be free of this life that had beaten him down, over and over. Yet, my heart ached. It wanted to leave and join him. If a heart can ever feel all things at once, mine was doing it in then.

How do I leave this room and my son's body? I paused and kissed him one last time on his forehead and eased away from his bedside. Seeing him for the last time, I turned and mechanically left the room.

I felt the connection to him yet separate at the same time. I was conflicted in the pain I was experiencing, but so happy for Michael.

I returned to a friend who was with me in the waiting room. He had spent time in the hospital with Michael a few days earlier. Tim is a rock that I needed.

A vision opened up again and I could see Michael standing. He was standing! My paraplegic son who hadn't stood since he was nine was standing! He was talking to a group.
"Mom, I can hear everything being said!" he told

me.

He showed me how he could hear the conversation I was having, while listening to the ones around him. He was amazed at this new ability. His hearing swiftly lessoned when he was 14, leaving him with 90percent hearing loss for most of his in life. Now, it was all restored and he was thoughtfully sharing it with me. I was excited for him, but at the same time, my heart was torn in the separation from his life in physical form.

This dance between both worlds was expanding my consciousness to new limits. Confused in the separation, my heart was numb and activated at the same time. The pain I was physically feeling wanted to take me to my knees and I knew I couldn't give into it in the moment. Tim walked me to the car. He put out his arms to hug me, but he didn't understand that if I let go there in the parking lot, I wouldn't be able to pull myself back together. I was left behind on earth and had to function until I was home safe and could let go.

I don't know how I got home. It was a 15-minute drive that the Angels must have made for me. Later that day, I called a second Tim who knew Michael. He came to my house, knowing loss through his own brother's passing. His kindness allowed me to let go and waves hit me all at once. There were ancient guttural sounds coming up from the depths of my entire being. Sobs wouldn't stop and my body was caving into it a vast emptiness. After hours, it was difficult to breathe. I needed space and looked to the river. It had been my peace in the past. Now more than ever, I needed its solace. It's all a blur, but somehow, we got into the river. I needed the water around me to hold me. I needed all of Mother Nature to hold me, the Universe to hold me. GOD and All that is GOD to hold me. It was the only place where I felt I could breathe. The three dogs, Tim, and I were in the water near the shore. I was sobbing into a greater pool of water and at the same time it represented the river's worth of tears I was crying.

The youngest puppy, Grace, began an odd behavior, something she had never done before. She went down into the shallows next to the shoreline, which was filled with rocks. Grace put her head under about 10 inches of water, coming up with rocks the size of golf balls, some even larger. Some of them she could barely put in her mouth. She went up the six or so steps to get from the water to the yard and laid it in the grass. She immediately went back down into the water and did the same thing again. She didn't acknowledge my voice when I called to her. She behaved as if she was on a mission. Over and over and over, her golden retriever eyes now sagging and looking waterlogged, she continued. She took all of the rocks one at a time from under the water and up to the grass.

I was concerned about her and got out of the water to stop her the next time she came out. I looked at the lawn. The rocks were laid out in a pattern in three very clear rows. Gracie's mission complete, she sat resting, exhausted. Abbi, her Jack Russell older sister, joined her and they both stared off to the side of the yard. I didn't see what they saw.

Grace never did that behavior again and she'd never done it before the day Michael transitioned.

That day the river held me allowed me the space for the entire day's events to sink in. My mind was numb, and my thoughts were consumed with Michael. This magnificent, genius, sweet-natured person who came into my life after 19 hours of two-minute contractions, born with the umbilical cord wrapped twice around his neck, who taught me unconditional Love, was gone from earth. The puppies knew without words.

The moment he was born, the greatest Love flooded my heart and overflowed. It's still that way today, missing him. My heart did not lessen when he let go of this world my with my hand over his heart feeling it beat, the other hand softly stroking his forehead, saying only words of Love to him and grateful for the time we shared together. That hand still feels his heart beating and the moment when it stopped.

Silence that happens in a mother's heart is deafening. It cried out for him and at the same time was grateful he didn't have to suffer any more. He had gone above and beyond to live life the best he could. People around him either understood his strength and loved him or resented his presence. Do people have such a fear it could be them in the wheelchair?

Michael lived as a warrior through everything that was thrown at him. Most of all, he was a Warrior of Peace and Love. He didn't want to have a funeral where everyone would grieve. He was Irish through and through. Instead, he said he wanted all to, "Raise a glass to my life!" I celebrate knowing him and holding him one last time, and giving him that final kiss on his forehead, thanking him for his Love.

Were the Angels there? In masses, the Angels attended. They held me up in the days that followed. They are with me now as I write and will be every day until my heart beats its final time. I pray I will be in the arms of someone who loves me to feel that kiss goodbye as I return to the Loving Source, knowing I will see Michael again.

Messages

Messages came from loved ones, especially in the first days. The one that came through Gracie in her unfamiliar behavior yet driven to accomplish

One came in flowers sent by a friend. A dear friend, Sue, sent the most beautiful pink roses to my home. They arrived in a vase and I sat them on the coffee table where they could be seen from any vantage point in the room. This was a few days after Michael's passing. When they arrived, a neighbor was with me to console and share of her loss. We both enjoyed their beauty and the thoughtful gesture.

I called Sue to say thank you. She was so kind as she listened and attempted to comfort me. I curled up in a big chair, it was the best place when no place felt right anymore. I mentioned sending her a photo of the roses earlier from my phone. In appreciation, I told her how my neighbor and I were touched by the beauty of pink roses.

Sue in her ever calm, soft way said, "Val, did you just thank me for pink roses?"

"Yes," I said and then stopped. "Sue, the roses aren't pink anymore. They're deep red! Minutes ago, they were bright pink...now they're red!"

We both became quiet. Something had just happened that we were probably going to keep to ourselves.

I'm sharing it now to show that there are reasons these odd things happen when someone passes. We do not need to understand. Please pause and take that moment, no matter what the message is. I call it a Divine Pause. Appreciate now, this minute in time. Smell the roses...pink or red.

The love continues after we say goodbye and miss a loved one's physical presence. The love just is. Michael said he loved me every day. No matter the age or situation, he was never embarrassed or shy about it. When he passed, I found my heart ached to hear his voice say one more time, "Mom, I Love you." About a week after he left, I was standing in the hallway at home when sobs began to pour out, as they did frequently, as I missed him so very much. Once again,

I yelled up to GOD/Source/Creator, "I miss him! I miss hearing "I Love You, Mom." Days and nights were spent unable to sleep, crying, unable to get a full breath, trying to make it through the day, even the next minute. Missing him...

Leaning against the wall next to the closet door something happened. I felt what I understand as energy shifting around me. I saw an opening happen in the air a few feet from me at heart level. A window, like before, had opened into that place. There came the unmistakable presence of Michael. I have no doubt it was him. He looked at me and said," I Love you, Mom." It was his voice and sounded exactly how I'd heard it every day when he was living on earth. It wasn't far off in the distance, nor was it a whisper. It was full, as if he was right there in the room with me. My heart felt he was.

He stayed very briefly, emitting so much love around and to me. He was holding me like no other could. The Angels were present, supporting the reunion. Our connection was Love and he was showing me the extent of the Love he now held. It was vast, beautiful, warm, encompassing Light, sweetness, wisdom, memories of joys flashing past, tender moments being relived in split seconds. The "I Love you, Mom" activated an overwhelming floodgate to open between us. The Universe could not deny the Love shared. Two Souls sharing a heart knowledge that allowed my heart to feel these loving expressions.

Michael and I shared many conversations over the last 10 years, as I explored and grew spiritually. We spoke of life and its purpose. To me, the message with the rocks was showing me that he understood it all now and was affirming the things we'd discussed at length. He's not physically present, and we are not separate.

In those long first days, messages continued. There was a pile of Michael's shirts before me, folded on the dining table. They were divided into stacks to give to friends who knew Michael.

At one point I picked up a long-sleeved green sweatshirt, his favorite color, and held it to my chest. He and I had never been able to dance standing. Wrapping one arm of the sleeve over my shoulder and holding the other out in my hand, I could smell his scent lingering. My extended right arm held the sleeve as I twirled around the wooden floor a few times, the shirt clinging to me. Tears flowed as I thought of all the things he never got to do. We had our dance.

One day when I laid down to meditate, I could feel his presence. He showed the images of me dancing with his green sweatshirt. It was like watching a movie of what went on days before. He saw it!

He was aware of everything I was feeling and going through. He was the stronger one now, looking after me and caring for me. I needed help and Michael was holding me up so I could go on. And with Michael's love and the Angel's love, I chose to go on.

Eight Years Later

I woke in the morning, knowing that this day marked eight years since Michael had passed. Changed inside and out, I had more lines on my face from rivers of tears. If we wear our lives on our faces, mine shows a woman who has lived and loved fully.

It was a quiet, thoughtful day, a day when my eyes watered without much thought. There are still moments with a vacant feeling across my chest. I reflected on our last evening together, discussing everything under the sun, being near him. I recalled his hand resting on top of mine as we spoke. How blessed I am to have those hours of memories of that last evening.

So much has happened the past eight years, so much healing.

A mother's heart breaks and everyone wants you to go on. Some expect it on a set timeline. What they don't realize, unless they experience it themselves, is that going on and continuing without your child, that part of your heart, is difficult on every level. Nothing is the same, NOTHING. I didn't even breathe the same. For me, it created more pauses in my day. Moments to reflect and remember.

When a thought of my son comes to me, I pause to be with it. It's been years and I still remember his touch, his voice, his laughter, him saying, "I love you, Mom."

What gifts he gave me. I pray that I will carry those memories always, for all time.

The memories are not heavy or a burden; they bring Light. His death was a shock to my system, no doubt. To this day I still feel his last heartbeats under my left hand resting on his chest. That final thump connecting to my pulse. Does my hand hold that memory, my mind, or my heart? It feels like all three do.

It's not so much about the last day anymore. There are bits of trauma around the situation, but that does not rule my life. It's healing. I think of these as lessons I don't want to forget.

What stands out are his birthdays. I always light a candle and sing "Happy Birthday" to him. It may sound silly. It always comes with a huge thank you to him for coming into this world through me, so we could have that amazing journey together. I celebrate him!

Sweet stories and memories come up now. Michael had lived near a busy street with a restaurant that had Karaoke on Friday evenings. He loved going there to sing. Yep, 90 percent hearing loss and he sang, what a spirit. He had retained memory of hearing and sang on key. His love of music included everything Celtic, singing in the brogue. It actually sounded pretty great.

One particular evening, he wheeled over to the restaurant and a wedding reception for a young couple was being held there. He took his usual place in line to sing. When he began to sing, the couple decided to have their first dance together. Afterwards, the groom came over to Michael and thanked him for making their wedding dance so special.

Michael didn't usually call me late unless it was an emergency health issue. When the call came that night, I was relieved to hear his voice so elated. He shared the groom's comments. His pride was coming through the phone.

"I was flying as I wheeled home," he said. That was a great night for Michael. The memory that makes me smile.

Just weeks after Michael's passing, my divorce was finalized. It was new and very lonely. The things I did were just filling time and a vast space. Coping was difficult, but I pushed myself to do anything to get out of the pain and yet it was always there. There is no escaping grief.

Holidays were also a tough time, so I stayed home most of the time. It wasn't easy for me to see others enjoying their families. I was happy they had each other, but I felt out of place. It seemed to work best when I spent all the holidays and birthdays with my three dogs. I was taking my time to heal. Being gentle in this process of my heart. Giving permission and time to heal was what I needed.

At first, going through the motions I knew that my heart was numb. New friends that shared a common spiritual connection found a way into my life. It was such a blessing having that supportive space. I am forever grateful to my girlfriends that carried me, along with the Angels.

Their strength held me up when I didn't have it in me. They listened to the stories I needed to share, so Michael would not be forgotten. They told their stories, too. A friend who had lost a daughter understood where my heart was. By telling the stories, in my mind, the Universe was hearing them and seeing how loved he was on Earth. He touched so many hearts. Even if you thought he was silly his heart was so huge it touched you.

My love letter to the Universe about my son is personal and every mother deserves to send her love message her own way. Grieving is a very tender, sacred process between child and mother.

Time gives us space between trauma and healing. I have tried not to linger in the trauma, although at times, it did hit me square in the face. All of the years of being involved with healers and taking on the role of assisting in healing for others gave me a strong base that helped immensely. Without it, I don't know how things would have gone. I'm grateful for all of the experiences that held me up in times I could not stand.

Until April 2020, I didn't know this story would include both of my sons. My writing is like my journal in elementary school—it was written down and left, written more to get me through, to work it out in my mind and heart.

My heart had taken the emotional hit of betrayal and my body chose to hold it in my gallbladder. My wonderful gallbladder had taken on all of my pain.

Looking back, I wonder if I was being looked after and prepared for a future event. If I hadn't realized what happened in this trauma with my gallbladder and learned from it, what would have happened when Michael died six months later? Would I have died from the loss?

It may have been too much for me to cope with, and I could not have gone on. I knew now to NOT take the pain inside, as I had done as a child. This experience allowed me to make another decision and break the cycle of my old survival tactics. What a lesson.

Learning from all that happens to us and around us is so important. These occurrences in our lives sometimes prepare us to go on. If we grow through challenges, we gain strength. That's my goal, to gain knowledge and move on with that to guide me forward. I think people forget that we are here for our Soul growth and that's it. I repeat this so you can better understand it and remember that you have a choice.

We didn't come here to see how many homes we can acquire or how many cars are in the driveway. We came for our Souls to experience and grow. Growth is not always happy, pretty, or easy. Growth can be gut wrenching, ugly, and heartache. The most growth comes in how we move through each challenge and what we choose to take from it.

Last winter I participated in an intimate workshop about trauma and understanding victimhood. I was sharing how we carry traumas from our childhood. Some wear it as a badge earned, deciding as a child to carry this trauma as "victim." As children, you don't know there are other options. Years pass and it grows heavier and heavier. They don't see that the child who went through the trauma has grown up and may choose to carry it or not. Trauma at a young age takes our power of choice until we realize that we are no longer the child. We have power but are fooled into believing that we didn't. How we look at the trauma aids in making a new choice.

Michael understood this, so did Scotty. I learned this in lessons. My mother didn't learn it while on earth. She and my youngest son, Nathan, gained their wisdom of it once leaving their bodies. There is hope for all to release traumas. I send love to everyone carrying childhood traumas. Healing can happen. May you be surrounded by Angels and move into healing, if you choose.

Putting Pieces Together

In the middle of the coronavirus, Covid-19, there is lock down in our country and the world. On April 17, 2020, my son Nathan went to the hospital in an ambulance. An hour later, I am told, he died of heart failure. Living alone, no partner, he had dealt with being sick with the flu for a couple of weeks isolated. Most likely he was not tested for the coronavirus, so we will never know. Nathan was 35 years old.

So many died during this tragic time, many alone. When I grieve, my thoughts go to all of the friends and families left behind. Were their loved ones alone? Were his last moments looking to strangers for help? Did someone hold his hand? I pray that the doctors, nurses, and EMTs caring for my son during his last hour of life were gentle, supportive, and showed him great kindness. They too are overwhelmed with this worldwide pandemic. How many faces do they look into or hold as a stranger passes in their arms? Too many.

Knowing Nathan as a grown man did not get to happen firsthand. He led a secretive life of alcoholism that I didn't know about. My son chose separation from me years ago and he wanted to stick to that choice. I wonder now how much alcoholism played a role in that.

Most people will not have cookie cutter lives where everything is perfect with flowers and love songs. Life has twists, turns, highs, and lows with challenges in it all. Our relationship suffered because of my choice. Then he chose to control it to the end. One of the hardest things in this life was honoring his wish for me to stay away.

Nathan was still in touch with my brother and a few nieces. Occasionally, a tidbit was shared with me. My family did not see the depth of my pain. I didn't want them to feel uncomfortable about their contact with Nathan. As long as someone was in contact with him, I was grateful.

The picture I can paint of him is up until he was

sixteen. I can hear his giggles as a toddler in my mind and see him as his big brother, Michael, read him a bedtime story. Nathan loved the water and was a natural swimmer. Michael nicknamed him "Thunder Kid," because when he was a toddler, he'd wake up from a nap and thump down the hall towards the family room, where Michael had built a tower from wood blocks for his baby brother to tumble down. He was silly and funny, tender and thoughtful. Nathan named his black Easter bunny Ernie. He loved all animals and they responded to him.

Nathan was creative, intelligent, and a gentle, kind, and loving spirit. Two of this first words were "tank you". He was such an angelic little boy, with a head of blonde curls that shifted to light brown as he grew. He loved to get into new things. He and I took up fishing when he was in middle school. The trips to streams and mountains were always special adventures. Crater Lake was a favorite place. Once we were joined by a deer who came for a drink a few feet from us. I loved watching him cast the line and stand there in the silence of nature.

When he fell in love with golf, he'd practice for hours working on his swing. And of course, always looking good. He was the only little guy who wanted to stop opening presents on Christmas morning when he opened gifts of clothes, so he could try them on. ALL of them! "Me on," he'd say.

He grew so fast and so tall. He loved looking down at all of us, putting an arm over our shoulders in a playful way.

I left and he did not want to come and live with me or visit. After that, he chose a side he didn't need to and that was the end. It was painful enough to be separated. Then to be cut off was so hurtful. My door was always open to him.

That's when mourning our relationship began. It was such a loss and yet he was alive. I cried every day for many years missing him. Grief isn't always death—it also happens in a disconnect. After years of praying and hoping for us to be close again, I realized that I needed to give it up to GOD and allow whatever was to happen. I had no control. All that I could do was love him from afar and pray he was watched over. My heart always ached for him and I gave that to GOD, too.

Nathan called me about twelve years ago. He wanted to talk. We chatted about his screen-printing job. It was fun hearing his excitement about something we both loved. He was excited about the creativity it involved. He told me he was surfing and shared a few stories. We were laughing. Then it all shifted. It happened like the snap of a finger. I heard him open a bottle and take a swig. Then another...and another.

I didn't think much of it until the conversation became cruel.

Seeing what was happening, I said, "Okay, why don't you say everything you need to and then we can work on healing and getting beyond the pain. I am here and listening." He kept pausing to take a gulp, what I assumed to be beer. He was also chain smoking, continually taking drags and lighting new cigarettes while he talked and drank. A new habit I had never witnessed him having.

We were both crying. My entire front of my sweatshirt sweatshirt was soaked through from snot and tears. The berating went on and on. I saw this as his younger, angry self. Next, he'd state that he didn't care and he wasn't angry anymore. I kept repeating, "I'm sorry. I cannot change any day in the past. I can only try to do better today." He wanted no part of that and took another swig.

I had a yellow pad to work through my issues. Nathan was dumping without resolve. There is a difference. I asked him if he could talk to a professional. He didn't feel he needed to; he was fine.

After what felt like hours, I said, "I'm sorry. Can we please begin right now with something new to find our way? Are you willing to do that?"

The person I knew he was inside was capable of this. This version of Nathan may not have been. He had to be the one to make the choice to move forward. He went back into the hurtful words. He couldn't see, or chose not to, the limits he created and was holding. What part did alcohol play in this?

"Nathan, this needs to be constructive and healing, not continuing the pain." With his ranting building again, I had to accept that this is where he was going to stay, for now.

"Nathan, I want to go on with you. This beating me up with your words needs to end. I can't accept abuse. Please know that I am always here if you want to go forward, if you want to talk so we can heal this. My door will always be open to you. I hope someday you will want to talk without the need to be cruel."

He wasn't hearing me.

His anger had increased, not defused.

"I have to hang up Nathan. Yelling at me is not serving anything. I love you, son. Good night." I gently hung up the phone.

It was so hard to do. Accepting the abuse to continue wasn't going to bring him to a point where we could find a resolution. It seemed to be fueling him deeper into his anger. After that night, Nathan went quiet. I would text with no response.

Over the years, my family all believed Nate was okay. His life wasn't easy, and he was making his own choices.

Since he passed, I've heard stories that have helped me put a picture together of him, as a man. No one in my family knew the degree of his alcoholism. They knew he partied and drank, but not to the extent he actually did.

After Nathan passed, his father, who I hadn't talked to in years, told me that Nathan had been in and out of rehab, had struggled, and that vodka destroyed his esophagus. How much vodka, at 35 years old, does it take to destroy an esophagus?

Reading the death certificate helped fill in more blanks. I knew his heart had stopped. He also had a rare kidney disorder and diabetes, due to the alcoholism. The sweet, caring, thoughtful, intelligent boy I raised went down a path that wrecked his body. He showed only bits and pieces of himself to people who loved him. If only we had known what was really going on. Would the love and support have been too much for him? As I heard these stories and listened to my nieces cry for him, I wondered if Nathan knew how loved he was?

I texted him over and over through the years without answers, except twice. One was about two weeks before he passed, asking him to be safe during this virus. He answered! Nathan answered! It was such a great day to hear from him. The next day I sent him a silly Jib-Jab video with family members filling the faces, mine included. I said it was to make him smile. I hope he did. I am forever grateful he answered. Did he sense something, and it was a way to say goodbye?

His last days, he was extremely ill and alone, spitting up blood. He had reached out, leaving a message for my niece, Jennifer, in Colorado to say, "I love you." I am grateful he did. She loves him so. Nathan made his way into many people's hearts. He is forever in mine. I Love You, Nathan, always will.

Heart Healing Further

In grieving, there are many stages. I grieved all of the years Nathan and I were apart. Over and over, I asked the Angels to look out for him. Even though there was this block he created between us, hearing of his death made me numb.

My niece, Heather, called to give me the news. When she said the words, my world stopped. I couldn't breathe. My chest hurt; my entire body ached.

I couldn't believe he was gone, that his adventure here was over so soon.

I realized how much of what I did was in hopes that someday he'd change his mind and want to see me again. It wouldn't need a discussion. Let's just be. That won't happen now. My heart hoped it would.

I still eat off the same dishes my kids used years ago. In case he ever showed up, it would be a way to let him know I was thinking of him with something familiar. A tile he painted when he was five is still on display. Little things so he would know he was never forgotten.

Why hang onto the dishes When it's almost painful to see them? My great hope was to see him before I died. I was patient and now, nothing. My heart hurts and is tired and worn.

Numb, it felt like there was an ancient sadness in every cell of my body. Two days after Nathan's passing, my partner, Pat's, father passed away at 91.
To try and explain what this planet is going through during the Covid-19 pandemic sounds unreal. It's more like a sci-fi movie than what we have all known as reality. Yet here it is. Masses of people dead in hospitals, others found dead in their homes. Testing is unorganized and no one knows the real truth of it all. The senior homes are shut down, everything is shut down, except for essential business. We shop for food online, then drive to the store parking lot to pick it up. We wear gloves and masks everywhere we go.

Funerals are not allowed. Immediate family may see the body in the casket. Pat's mother, a grieving widow in her eighties, couldn't come to the burial in case she had been exposed to Covid-19 herself. Instead, we live in a time when she used FaceTime watch her beloved husband's casket being closed. My heart was breaking for her and the family. She didn't get the hugs we all need for comfort. She was in lockdown, isolated at a senior living facility.

At the cemetery, everyone wore masks and respectfully stood six feet apart. We stood at the grave now covered with fresh dirt, but no marker yet. There were prayers and a few sweet stories from the children, now grown and in their sixties. I was supportive of Pat, standing by his side. Standing at the foot of the grave, it hit me. It took all of my strength to keep it together as my thoughts went to Nathan, who had died one week earlier. Who was going to be at his burial?

My only task had been to sign papers so he could

be cremated. I was told his ashes would not be put in a grave. Instead, when the restrictions are lifted on the beaches in California, his ashes will be released at his favorite beach. Nathan loved the ocean, he loved water. It feels right that his body has the freedom to join the waves and find the peace it always brought him.

Those first few days, I didn't see a reason to go on. Not everyone understands that I felt I could die. Once the numbness wore off, I began to feel the heartache down to my toes. I wasn't drawing from him, yet him being on the planet, even in separation, there was a force of mother child love going on. When Michael died it nearly destroyed me. Now with Nathan's death, what was the point in continuing?

For days, it felt like my body was ready to give in. My blood pressure was spiking and everything about my body felt as if it could shut down. Why live? Searching my heart, it turned to Pat. We had united in 2018 as friends. After over 40 years of separate lives and experiences, both knowing our own versions of love and loss, the love we shared together is what kept me here. It holds me in this time. I am so grateful. Did the Angels help us find each other for this time? I wouldn't be surprised.

This loss around Nathan is so different. With Michael I was right there and so connected and present with him. With Nathan, I heard after he had already passed. His ending felt empty. Thank goodness for the Angels. I know they were holding both of us.

When hearing of Nathan's passing, I opened up my intuition and all I could see was a tall brilliant light Source. The flowing Light was vibrant and charged, and so white, the whitest of whites. It glowed with nothing around it. When I tried to connect with him, this glow is all I could see. It was almost blinding. No details of him. No words, just that Light. I trusted that this image was all I was to see and let go. If there was to be more, it would happen.

At first, I thought the Light might be a doorway

opened for all of the people worldwide who were passing during this pandemic. Time has taught me I don't need to know everything. I have learned to see what I see when I see it, and let the rest go.

A day or so passed, jumbled in the little sleep, not eating much, sharing with people. Hours of crying and looking through old photos was a way of saying goodbye. I was going through the motions needed in everyday life once again. It was all puzzling. Was that it? No message from Nathan? Sadly, not hearing from him had become accepted. The only thing I was sure of was that the Angels had to be carrying me. There was also that steady love from Pat that I have learned to accept and lean on. During the long discussion with Michael on his last night, he told me to find a good man. I did.

Transmission of Love

When I woke in the middle of these long nights, I'd leave the bedroom so that I wouldn't disturb Pat. Two days before Mother's Day, I went out to the living room to sit on the straight back sofa to cry, as I did most nights these days.

The room has lovely energy of amethyst cathedrals, Selenite, and a rose quartz heart. It feels good to sit there. A foot massager is in place that I've grown to rely on to ease my foot pain. I'm still dealing with RSD, which happened before Michael's passing.

Sitting in the dark with a box of tissues while my feet were being manipulated, I wept. Soon, the tissue was drenched. I allowed myself to feel everything that came up, all memories happy and sad.

It must have been rough on Nathan having a brother with so many health issues. I did my best to make time and give special attention to Nathan. Only he knows what he felt and experienced. It was sad that

Nathan also created a separation between himself and his brother years ago. Maybe he felt abandoned by both of us when Michael came to live in Michigan. Nathan didn't want to leave California and I had to respect that.

All of these thoughts and so much more came, one after another. We missed so much together. It's sad when years of missed opportunities stack up, one on top of another.

In allowing the tears to flow, I felt I could avoid storing my grief in my body, as I'd previous done with my gallbladder. I had learned my lesson. It wasn't a pretty cry, but it didn't matter. My nose leaked as much as my eyes. The rims became sore and probably swollen. I didn't look in the mirror much. My entire body sobbed, sometimes yawing in between them. I knew I had to get this out.

My lap was filled with soaking-wet, balled-up tissues. The house was silent, except for the massager moaning as it held my feet. Pat's light snoring came from the bedroom. How I love that sound.

I breathed deeply. The tears subsided briefly. I was beginning to get sleepy when the Angels came around me. Something always happens when a group of Angels show up. Instantly my body goes into complete ease. That was a great relief that night. It grounded me. I soaked it up and sat quietly, appreciating them all.

The Angels moved out to make way for the Grandmothers to take their place around me. It's always an exchange that happens with such grace. Over the years, I became familiar with appearances from the Grandmothers. It's always very loving and supportive. It felt like they welcomed me into the wisdom they carry. What an honor. They understood the loss I was feeling. It was a knowing we all shared, and I knew they had come to hold me.

To someone who has no understanding of the Angels or Grandmothers it's a challenge to explain. It is a trust, as I trust GOD, the Creator, is fully present in my heart. This love is not limited to that energy. I believe GOD/Source/Creator gives us supports for our earthly lives with these extensions of Love energies. Simply put, to me, the Grandmothers represent femininity and motherhood.

I've always known God's Love and the loving messages I receive. I've been carried through the worst of times and know that this is the purest origin of all that is Love.

It felt sacred being held by the feminine energies of the Grandmothers. The words, again, came in a transmission. Unspoken yet, my mind or heart deciphered their intent. It was as if giving birth was the first initiation into this group. It was being revisited on a new level because I felt the circle complete for my child's life, my children's lives. They could feel the depths of my pain. There is a kinship, a feminine unity.

In this expanded circle of wisdom, my body relaxed into a knowing. Such quiet from beyond this intimate moment. Gratitude filled me and washed over me. The air in the room had changed and I could hear their joined voices expressing sounds and vibrations that carried me.

They were the same waves as Love that I'd received that night on the sofa when the TV became static and I heard an energy clearly for the first time. TV screens were no longer needed. The same gentleness is still there, easing to me so my delicate human body can accept this higher vibration. They seemed to prepare or fine tune me, immersing me in waves of love. It has become familiar as my own heartbeat.

What's this all about, I wondered. Was I exiting and they were my greeters? I waited, fully present in their love. Sad tears had stopped. What was flowing felt so sacred, an awesome pure gift.

In the softness of it all, bouquets of flowers began appearing at my feet. Beautiful flowers of brilliant colors, so perfect. A Light seemed to bring them. I don't remember smelling them. So much was happening at once. Another bouquet appeared...and another, being laid at my feet. Was this an Angel bestowing these armfuls of flowers? Was this all a part of the sendoff? If this is it, this is a wonderful way to go.

Then I felt him. I felt Nathan's presence. It wasn't the boy I knew who had created a separation from me. This was a mature energy, carrying that same sweetness that is only him. He came as a Light, but unmistakably him. I knew it with everything in me. Slowly it seemed to glide towards me. When close enough, he leaned into my right shoulder and whispered gently into my ear, "Happy Mother's Day, Mom." It was a bit of a shock hearing this because this was the first time he acknowledged me as mom since he was seventeen. The word mom I have missed so very much. I ached to hear it and there he was saying it. Again, he whispered those words I was hoping to hear one day. "Happy Mother's Day, Mom," his voice the same as I remembered. Nathan was a tall man about 6'4" with a voice that came from his toes.

The same tone, same rhythm he spoke in before. And now I was hearing it again. He repeated it over and over, sweetly with a loving intent that was clear and gentle. Finally, he said, "This is for all of the Mother's Days I missed." The wave of love he was sending me overwhelmed my body and all of senses. There came a rush of years of unsaid words. Anything that was not of that love was gone. Any separation vanished in the rush of wave of love.

He was free and now that gift was being given to me by the only one who could give it. My face was wet from the tears.

Nathan, I love you so much!!! I screamed from my heart to the universe.

Tears left my nightshirt wet, everything flowing. He came back to heal me. This precious Being that was so angelic as a child had returned to heal my pain.

Time passed and things were said between us. The conversation is lost in those moments. Maybe too private to ever share with others. Precious sweet moments opened up for the two of us to share. What an extraordinary gift of love.

Recently, I told someone that I wished Nathan and I would have shared one last hug. Nathan leaned over putting his arms around me. Holding each other so tight he whispered, "I'm sorry, Mom." He kept holding me. Michael's energy came in and the three of us hugged together. My heart was healing so deeply in this connection. I heard and felt I Love You from my sons. My entire being became my heart. It seemed we were in a time of no time because nothing else mattered.

Gently, Michael moved away. We are always connected so it wasn't a loss when he did. They must have sensed my exhaustion from this magnificent transmission of love and healing. Nathan began releasing sweetly and eased away. I didn't feel desperate to hold onto him, its beyond that now. We are reconnected and I could feel this was not the end. This was our new beginning. In bliss, I sat thanking that Angels and Grandmothers who held the space and witnessed, as they do in all things.

This was one of the most beautiful sacred moments in this life. One that will be with me forever. I remember feeling the tiredness in my body and I went to bed. It was the first night I'd slept since he passed.

When I awoke the next day, there was something lifted. I missed Nathan. There are so many levels of grief between a child and mother—Spiritual, Physical, Emotional...each one takes time.

The next night I woke up crying. Slowly moving out of bed, I headed to my familiar spot on the sofa. He came again and for the next few nights. There were no Grandmothers or bouquets, Just the same waves of love filling the room. The Angels prepared a space for us to meet each time. It was just Nathan and me. We talked undisturbed. I asked questions and was more mentally conscious of the exchange. He was so present, yet no longer in earth's physical body form. We laughed a few times over memories, and I called him Natie Nu, which I did when he was young. This night was more joyful in a different way. We spent hours together. I wanted to stay as long as I could with him, to be near him. He'd give me a look and I headed back to bed, knowing I needed to rest.

This same pattern continued for three nights. The last night, the Angels again came close. Waves of love filled the room and Nathan arrived. I brought up things that had hurt me. I expressed what I was holding inside, and he listened intently at every word, never a judgment, never an excuse. It was as if a most wise Being was there to lift the heaviness I carried. I must have been searching inside into every nook and cranny. It was all said calmly. He even asked me a few things that unearthed subjects I hadn't thought of. It was a gift on a different level. Our relationship shifted that night. It was two beings figuring things out, instead of mother and child. I am forever grateful.

Pat was at work when I woke the following morning. When I opened my eyes, Nathan appeared at the side of the bed and sat down. He leaned toward me and said, "I'm going now, Mom." He stayed for only a minute or two. I don't remember what we said. It was more of just being. I felt us hugging, saying another lifetime of words in a transmission of love. And he was gone.

Tears continue, showing up out of nowhere and at unscheduled times and places. It's been months now. The tears have come every day while writing, but they are no longer holding me in a pattern of a sad ending. They're releases; clearing, healing, and helping free my physical body from the trauma of loss. More came up with Michael, too.

My sons were two different beings, two different personalities. Both challenged and both are my greatest teachers and healers. What I have grown to understand and accept through them and their journeys, has taken me into understanding and wisdom I never could've imagined.

To be the mother of these extraordinary beings, to love them and feel their love in return beyond this earth plane is what I carry forward. It's a quiet knowing and deeper connection that carries me, a love language.

Letters

Dear Souls,

If you have lost a child from any reason, I am so deeply sorry for your loss. Your heart opened when you gave birth, adopted, or cared for a child of any age. Our hearts do not discriminate. When we love, we love. I believe we are designed that way.

We have the physical heart that aches for our children because of that sacred connection that happens in us. When a child dies, our heart feels as if it is literally fracturing off and breaking. The same thing happens when our own mothers leave Earth. It happens in a different way. It is the bond that is being disrupted from living on Earth with us. The connection is broken, just the energy binding us to Earth thins and ends. The true sacred connection gets stronger, even when you do not feel it.

Knowing this information does not take away the pain. My hope is that you trust that your connection is not broken. Trust that they hear you. Trust that they see your pain and know the truth of it. Trust that one day when you leave here you will look again into those eyes—eyes that turned to you for guidance, to say I love you, or to say goodbye.

Women have been giving birth, caring for children, and burying them for all time. As we become more conscious, we are closer to them more than ever before. Do we miss them? Every day. We learn to go back out into the world knowing what this is. The world keeps going, even when it feels like ours is falling apart. It's okay if you feel you are in slow motion. It's okay if you need to continue for others. Just take time each day before you close your eyes to tell them you love them. I yelled it out to the entire Universe to hear. Do it in any way you need to.

Please don't push your pain down. Pain pushed down turns into dis-ease in your body, as I experienced with my gallbladder. Try writing letters or emails to yourself. Tell the stories you want to be remembered to friends and family, if they are kind enough and open to hear them. You have a story to tell. Your heart has a story to tell. If inclined, ask your

Angels to hold you. Ask them to be close and guide you; they will. They know all of your stories, so tell them. Trust that they are there for you. They never tire of listening.

Give yourself permission to grieve. You may have a need to do it different then another person and that's okay. Remember, it is a very sacred time and your need to morn is important. Being stuck in it does not keep them alive. Healing and remembering them, keeps them alive in our hearts. Even if you lose a child before birth, there's a memory of carrying your baby. Your body knows it and will need time to grieve and heal.

I am blessed to see and feel expressions and that's what I've shared with you. If you're not yet able to do this, set the intention to receive a sign. Signs come in many different ways. When we pause and are still it's amazing what can happen. Signs are around us every day.

My dog even showed a sign. Animals or insects may

come to you. A light may flicker, or a phone or alarm ring. You may come across something that touches you deeply and connects you with that child. Even a stranger may give you a message that only you will understand. Or there will be silence because that is how you best receive healing. You are unique.

My life has been focused on healing for almost 20 years. How perfect that my sons came to heal me. What an awesome gift they shared. My hope is that you find that message and that your heart begins to heal in the most gentle of ways surrounded by Light. My prayer is that people around you show kindness and give you the space and love you need to begin and continue your healing process. May you receive healing in ways that you need and release the pain.

My final hope is that you trust and have faith in your love as a mother, sister, father, brother, knowing that you were a part of a wonderful, bright being's experience in this world, whether for a day or 80 years. I wish you Great Love, Val

First Mother's Day -

I am blessed with Bri, the dearest goddaughter a woman could wish for. My youngest brother, Bobby, gave me this heart treasure. She's like the daughter I never had. Now she has precious, Luke. Thank you, Bobby, I Love You.

Mother's Day was weeks after Nathan's passing. It was a tough day to make it through. Pat my Sweetheart, being conscious of what the day was for me, made it low key. People were being tender in messages. It's still Covid and social distancing, so no hugs from anyone but Pat. I just wanted to breathe and get past the day.

A text came in the evening. "Aunt Val, go to the window and wave."

My niece, along with her mom, my brother, and her son were all in sitting in a car in the driveway. She surprised me with beautiful roses and candy that she left for me on the front porch. My heart ached missing my family and there they were. I ran out to them wanting to hug each of them and couldn't because we all needed to stay safe. They all lived together so they could have contact. Pat and I stood outside the car and we all talked for a while. Just seeing them inside the car helped my heart so much! I am forever grateful for that wonderful loving gesture. Mother's Day ended in a way I could not have expected.

Through my friends, brother, all nieces and their children, and through Pat with his children, I have family and Love.

What's Next & Book Cover

The Angels will forever be a part of my day, my choice. Why some people feel or hear them and others don't, it's about your experience here, it's not about judgement. We all came in for our Soul's growth and not all growth includes seeing and hearing Angels.

I apparently am supposed to see them. This lifetime would've been so much more traumatizing without them. Maybe my Soul needed handholding through this one.

The cover for this book was guided by the Angels. This painting was one of the many lessons in listening. One day, while in a craft store, Angels told me to buy art painting supplies. I told them I didn't know how to paint. They went into the familiar ever-patient mode. It ended with me picking up on their message and buying a few supplies. After about a year of repeated guidance to purchase supplies, there was an assortment of everything a person could need to paint.

Out of the blue one morning, guidance came, "Paint!"

"But I don't know how to paint," I repeated. See how our relationship continues.

I was standing at the easel in the kitchen, waiting. The Angels began to show me the colors I was to use. I placed a few squirts from the tubes of each. I stood there waiting. One came forward, I wonder if they drew straws. A lovely Angel pointed to a wide brush, followed by guidance for each color to blend.
Step by step, I was shown what color to put on each area on the once blank, white canvas.

This turned into me feeling the strokes and playing in it. "I don't think that color works there," I said. Again, the quiet, patient look came, and I did what I'd been guided to do. I have never said I don't question. You would think they would have figured this out by now. :)

To my amazement and complete delight, after many strokes of the brush things began to appear! "I see it!" The Angels smiled as I happily shared the painting. It's funny looking back at how silly I was. When finished, the Angel said in that ever-sweet tone, "That is your Heart."

Of course, I cried. It was so touching and kind that helped me express it. What a gift they gave that day. And now it seems so prefect to have it on the cover of this book, telling a story from my heart. Thank you, Angels, I Love you!

May the Angels guide all my future paintings and writing. I have already begun a series of fiction books that are explorations into imagination and a different reality. It will be fun to see where that goes.

There are dozens of stories that occurred between 1985 and 2020. I imagine they will continue until the end of my life. I've tried to share over the years, so others could feel the connection and heal.

In 2020, it seems it is required that all find their own way from within themselves. That is the best road to take. Empowering you, by pausing and finding that voice and sensing your answers. To find your answers in someone else takes your journey and puts it in their hands, not yours.

No one is perfect. That is why we're here to learn and grow. Anyone who is intuitive, senses, feels, hears, and deciphers Angelic Source knowledge through their own expressions from their lives and their own trauma. You may get a clearer message yourself. It's all free will and you get to choose your path.

Please know, if you don't feel the connection, it's okay. Most people are receiving love and wisdom often but are not conscious of it. I'm a strong believer in the Divine Pause. Whatever it is you choose to believe is okay. None of this is about judgment.

When I yelled at the Angels and God that they either be in my life all of the time or not at all, I trusted that I was being heard. I was—and it's been one heck of a journey. I'm blessed and excited about the future.

In everything there is a lesson. My sons have turned out to be my greatest teachers and healers. They taught me love and all aspects of it. Only they could've taken me into the depths we traveled. Gratefully, I get to carry the wisdom of them forward in all I do.

I now understand my emotions and why I'm set up the way I am. I was deeply affected when my baby brother was born dead. That loss created a wound in my heart that I unconsciously tried to fill. That began to shift, when instead of filling the wound, my focus went to healing it. With new understandings, that part of me is being continuously loved. Our hearts are sacred precious parts of us. It takes time to heal a wounded or broken heart.

My mother struggled with having a sensitive, needy five-year-old girl. She was doing her best. I was in a place of not only losing a baby brother, but losing my mom, too. As a child, it was incredibly sad. The whole house changed and I became lost not only from the death, but other things that were happening in the household. My Spirit was muted.

The trauma shut down parts of me yet ignited something else. It opened the nurturer in me. Circumstances happened that made me a protector and nurturer for others. We give out what we really need ourselves. I needed protecting. I needed to be nurtured.

Years later, workshops, therapies, and study, helped me understand that part of me. This understanding and healing made me stronger in ways people could not see. It's a shame that sensitivity was not seen as a positive asset. Mine may have been muted a bit. Thank goodness it never stopped. It grew and continues to grow. In the search, I discovered I could nurture myself, as well as others.

We are magnificent Souls stopping by for an array

of advanced lessons. We can grow in challenges on earth, or not. The opportunity is in our face every day. For years I prayed, asking for patience. Michael was always in the hospital, rehab, or therapy. Year after year, many, many lessons taught me patience. I received exactly what I prayed for. I can laugh about it now and am more discriminatory in my prayer requests. All of these life challenges are lessons in one way or another.

As I age, having watched my parents time here come and go, my point of view has shifted. Close friends and family become most important. Having little ones around is so healing. It nurtures my heart. I'm able to give them the love and attention to make them know they're special.

What we do and say to a child matters. Every child deserves someone on their side to make them feel special. I had one in my grandfather from New York. Our adoration was mutual. He was my special someone. His love, kindness, and respect saved me. Thank you, Grandpa.

My sons are gone and my life is filled with all of these wonderful people. Because of everything I've lived through, I know how to love and be loved. I know a level of peace. What a glorious time to watch everyone beginning their own adventures. I am so fortunate every day.

Each step of the way we can heal, or not. It's up to us. No one has a perfect life. Each challenge shapes who we are. We're in charge of our reaction and what we decide to take from each challenge. Free will is a gift to activate the choice of your response to all challenges. Reaction is working from a past choice. Response is now, in the consciousness you hold today.

There are so many changes happening in the United States and around the world. Where we end up is up to us. What are we preparing for our children to inherit? Will they come away with our traumas or our healing? That is up to each of us to choose. What wisdom will we leave behind to awaken the young ones in your life? What story will you leave behind?

My Heart has loved, lost, grown, and expanded into healing beyond the initial grief. This does not mean that I still don't cry and miss them everyday, I do. I'm grateful for discovering new understandings.

I have been guided to complete something that I've been working on over the years. **_The new book talks about the Spiritual aspect of Transitioning. It will be out in 2021_** to help further understand and explore the process of passing beyond earth, and how to heal and remain when a loved ones do not.

May all love come into your life in expressions that give you peace, open your heart, and help you heal beyond loss. May you find comfort and joy, and discover the wisdom waiting for you.

Tell your heart story. It's perfect if it's your truth. Thank you for reading mine.
With great love, Val

VAL22280@gmail.com
I am here

www.ingramcontent.com/pod-product-compliance
Lightning Source LLC
Chambersburg PA
CBHW032120090426
42743CB00007B/415